D1394974

CROQUET

THE
COMPLETE
GUIDE

CROQUET

THE

COMPLETE

GUIDE

A. E. Gill

HEINEMANN KINGSWOOD

100743806

Heinemann Kingswood
Michelin House, 81 Fulham Road, London SW3 6RB

LONDON MELBOURNE AUCKLAND

First published 1988
0 434 98100 1

Printed and bound in Great Britain by
Butler & Tanner Ltd., Frome and London

To my dear wife Nicola, who has peeled
me through so many of life's difficult hoops

CONTENTS

Acknowledgements   xiii
Introduction   xv

PART ONE

 1 Beginnings   3
 2 The Victorians   14
 3 The outposts of Empire and beyond   32
 4 Transatlantic croquet   38
 5 Sphairistike and resurrection   44
 6 Croquet personalities up to date   54
 7 Social croquet   68
 8 Croquet observed   76

PART TWO

 9 John Jaques & Son   89
10 Where to play   98
11 Lawn and equipment care   103

PART THREE

12 Dress   113
13 The court and equipment   117
14 The game   126
15 Tactics and practice   142

16 Handicaps and peeling   153
17 Variations on a theme   158
18 The last word   174

APPENDICES

Appendix A: Croquet equipment   179
Appendix B: Croquet abroad   182
Appendix C: Principal clubs in Eire, Great Britain and the
             USA   184
Appendix D: Principal UK tournaments, and the Mac-
             Robertson Shield   187
Appendix E: The Basic Laws of Association Croquet   190

Glossary   201
Bibliography   203
Index   205

LIST OF ILLUSTRATIONS

Plates

1	The golf stroke in the game of pall-mall	7
2	A pall-mall court from an eighteenth-century book	8
3	Mallets and their forebears	9
4	An example of crinoline croquet	11
5	Walter Jones Whitmore	15
6	A rare set of Squails	17
7	Chastleton House	20
8	*The Croquet Queen* – frontispiece to Captain Mayne Reid's book	25
9	'Croquet'd he was completely' – the first cartoon about croquet	27
10	'Croqué'd' – a cartoon from *Punch*	27
11	A croquet arch	28
12	Tight croquet	30
13	'How we play Croquet at Buddleapoor!'	33
14	HH The Maharajah Gaekwar of Baroda playing croquet in front of his palace	34
15	A Chinese communist guerilla prepares a rush	37
16	*Summer in the Country*, Winslow Homer	39
17	Jack Osborn	41
18	An 1870s advertisement for Lawn Tennis, or 'Sphairistike'	46
19	The first *Croquet Gazette*, 1904	49
20	Miss Lily Gower	50
21	An Edwardian advertisement – Table Croquet	51

22	Miss D D Steel	52
23	The MacRobertson Shield	55
24	Humphrey Hicks, using side style	57
25	John Solomon and Monty Spencer Ell	58
26	Keith Wylie, Northern Championship, 1983	59
27	John Solomon	61
28	Lionel Wharrad	63
29	Nigel Aspinall, winning final of mixed doubles championship, 1982	64
30	Liz Taylor	65
31	A croquet tournament at Highgate in 1869	69
32	Croquet at the Duke of Richmond's castle, 1860s	70
33	The game of Croquet, from *Alice's Adventures Under Ground*	78
34	*Partie de Croquet*, Edouard Manet	80
35	*A Game of Croquet*, Winslow Homer	80
36	*Croquet*, James Tissot	81
37	*A Game of Croquet*, John Nash	82
38	Thomas Jaques' business card	90
39	John Jaques I	92
40	John Jaques II	92
41	John Jaques V and Christopher Jaques	92
42	Lignum vitae, to be made into croquet mallet heads	95
43	Mallets from a Jaques catalogue of 1910	97
44	Nigel Aspinall winning final of Men's Championship, 1983	100
45	Richard Rothwell	105
46	A target, from a Jaques catalogue of 1931	110
47	A German illustration of ladies' clothing	114
48	Dressed to croquet in the thirties	114
49	Very casual croquet in the twenties	115
50	Dr Roger Wheeler with Hugh Carlisle	116
51	The perfect setting for the game	118
52	A good croquet set for the serious player	121
53	A selection of modern mallets	123
54	Side stance	128
55	Hoop running	128
56	Standard grip, US version, front view	129
57	Standard grip, US version, side view	129
58	Standard grip, British version, front view	130
59	Standard grip, British version, side view	130
60	Solomon grip, front view	130

61	Solomon grip, side view	130
62	Irish grip, front view	131
63	Irish grip, side view	131
64	Stephen Mulliner	156

Diagrams

Fig. 1	Standard court and setting	119
Fig. 2	Two sorts of rush	133
Fig. 3	Running a hoop	134
Fig. 4	Three croquet strokes	136
Fig. 5	Three rolls	137
Fig. 6	A simple split shot	138
Fig. 7	An opening	143
Fig. 8	(a) 2-ball break	
	(b)	
	(c)	145
Fig. 9	(a) 3-ball break	
	(b)	
	(c)	146
Fig. 10	(a) 4-ball break	
	(b)	
	(c)	
	(d)	
	(e)	147
Fig. 11	A leave	150
Fig. 12	Leaving Red and Yellow 'wired'	150
Fig. 13	American 'Backyard' croquet	166
Fig. 14	Layout of court for 'Croquet Castles'	171

ACKNOWLEDGEMENTS

Croquet is enjoying a revival at the moment, and nothing provides better proof of that than the number of people who play it. I talked to a great many of them, and I can say that without their generous help I could never have written this book. I owe particular thanks to: G N Aspinall, the world's Number One player; Anne Bates, Administrative Assistant of the United States Croquet Association; Enrique F de Bobadilla; Dennis Bulloch, Publicity Officer of the New Zealand Croquet Council; Veronica Carlisle; Paula Chesterman, librarian of *Punch*; Barbara Clutton-Brock, of Chastleton House, who lent me all of Walter Jones Whitmore's surviving manuscript papers, as well as an unpublished history of Chastleton by her late husband, Professor Alan Clutton-Brock, with its valuable chapters on Walter Jones Whitmore and others of the Whitmore Jones family; Mary Collin; Brian Coupe; Norman Eatough; Morgan Entrekin, the United States' 'most improved player' of 1985; Gary Fisketjon; Caroline Funnell; Ian Gillespie, President, the South African Croquet Association; Ashley Heenan, OBE, President of the New Zealand Croquet Council; Donald Hodge; Marjorie Hodge; Chris Husdon, Development Officer of the Croquet Association; Christopher Jaques, Managing Director of John Jaques & Son, who showed me all the intricacies of croquet equipment manufacture, and who generously lent me books and items from Jaques' private museum, including a set of 'Squails'; Sue Leighton; Sir Michael Levey; Alan Little, Librarian, the Kenneth Ritchie Wimbledon Library; Brian Macmillan, Administration Secretary, the Croquet Association; Miss Meade; Chris Moller; Gillie Morley; Andrew Hope, Chairman of

Council, the Croquet Association; Professor B G Neal, former Chairman of Council, for much help and hospitality, and even a demonstration of technique; David Neville; Sally Neville; Jack Osborn, President, the United States Croquet Association; the late D M C Prichard, former Chairman of Council; R F Rothwell, former Chairman of Council, first full-time professional Secretary of the Croquet Association, and fifty years a player; John Stanton, for drawing my attention to Victorian music-hall songs of the 1860s and early 1870s on croquet; J W Solomon, President of the Croquet Association, for much valuable advice and for allowing me to borrow his unpublished *Personal Croquet History*; J V Stevenson; Charles Townsend, Managing Director of Townsend Croquet Equipment; Jane Turnbull; Stephen Warren; Valerie Warren, Curator, the Wimbledon Lawn Tennis Museum; Lionel Wharrad, former Chairman of Council, the Croquet Association; M R Wormald; I Howard Wright, Secretary, the Scottish Croquet Association; Keith Wylie, and Frances Yorke Batley.

I am indebted to E L Gill for background research, to Mary-Lou Grimberg for editing my manuscript so well, and to the staff of the British Library, London.

INTRODUCTION

Croquet is an intellectually demanding game which requires a
high level of dedication and concentration to play well. Given that, it
is immensely rewarding. It taxes your patience, but it *teaches* you patience
too, and also that, no matter how desperately lost the battle may seem
to be, your fortunes can turn at the last minute.

My reasons for writing this book are twofold: to introduce the
game to the beginner or would-be player, and to provide some knowledge of its history to the enthusiast who would like to know more.
An authoritative history of the game by the late D M C Prichard was
published some years ago, but it is no longer readily available. On
completing the present book I turned to Prichard to check one or two
facts, and found that inevitably he and I had covered some of the same
ground; but I decided not to cut out what I had already put in because
the present book is aimed at the general reader, who may not wish to
refer to so esoteric a work as Prichard's.

For my own historical research, especially in relation to Walter
Jones Whitmore, I have been lucky enough to have a personal contact
through my mother with Barbara Clutton-Brock, the present owner of
Chastleton House, and the widow of Professor Alan Clutton-Brock, a
descendant of the Whitmore Jones family. Barbara gave me free access
to her late husband's unpublished memoir of Chastleton, and to all of
Walter Jones Whitmore's papers – an invaluable source. Many months
were also spent tracking down material in the British Library. Brian
Macmillan, Administration Secretary of the Croquet Association,
allowed me generous access to the collection of croquet books in his

office, none of which, sadly, have remained in print, and few of which are readily available elsewhere. I have had much help from prominent people in the croquet world at home and abroad, and I thank them in the Acknowledgements. It goes without saying that any faults in the text are not theirs, but my own.

Croquet is not a game that need necessarily be played too seriously or at club level, though if you are bitten by the croquet bug and feel driven to improve your skill, you will do this best by joining a club (details of how to are given later) to widen your choice of opponents. However, it is a game that rewards proper play, and if there is a third purpose for my book it is to set the record straight as far as the rules of the game are concerned for the private player who may still believe in such horrors as putting your foot on the ball.

Another couple of myths I might as well get rid of immediately are that croquet's a game for the rich (the 'cucumber sandwich' syndrome), and that it's vicious. Croquet may have been a game for the leisured classes a hundred years ago, but that is simply no longer the case. People from all walks of life play nowadays. The only essential in a croquet player is an ability to concentrate and to keep cool. Without this, you'll find the game frustrating and irritating, and you should find something else to do. In practice, most people who play croquet tend to enjoy thinking things out, to be problem solvers, and to have logical, strategic imaginations.

As for the old chestnut about the game being vicious; well it is and it isn't. When you are on a winning streak and have your opponent on the run, you can give your killer instinct free rein and *slaughter* him. Which is fun. He'll do the same to you given the chance – the losing player can come up from behind with bewildering and devastating implacability. So be prepared for an emotionally charged afternoon and, as I said above, try not to become too overwrought! However, all games are about winning, and consider: is it vicious for a bowler to get a batsman out, or for a tennis player to serve an ace?

Croquet has the advantage over other games that more or less anyone can play anyone else, regardless of sex or age. An eighty-year-old woman can play a twenty-year-old man and win, for the game doesn't principally require great physical strength. It does demand durability, though, because it's played in all weathers, a game can last three hours, and you can find yourself standing for protracted periods.

Bending to the mallet can tax your back, though some back-sufferers have found the side style (see later) easier than the centre style.

There has been a number of versions of the game, but its proper form today is defined in the 'International' Laws of Association Croquet, according to which it is played in Europe, Australia, New Zealand and South Africa; and the Official Rules of the United States Croquet Association, which differ slightly. Whenever I use the unadorned word 'croquet' I'll be referring to one or other of these standard games. Variations are dealt with in a separate chapter, but learn the real rules first. They will introduce you to a game which is complex, stimulating and fun. It's beyond me why some people think it's boring – but maybe they've just watched a game once without understanding what's going on. That's enough to make anything seem dull.

Like all other games, croquet has its own specialised jargon which you'll need to know the basics of. There is a glossary at the end of the book, but two words you must learn immediately are *roquet* and *croquet*. You make a *roquet*, after which you must take *croquet*. This sequence is the cornerstone of the game.

Roquet: in some ways croquet is like snooker or billiards, insofar as you use one ball to hit others with. You hit your own ball with the mallet, aiming it at another ball. If you hit that ball, you've *made a roquet.* What happens next is the unique feature of croquet: the *croquet stroke.* You can *only* use this after you've made a roquet, and then you *must* use it.

Croquet: having made your roquet, you *pick up* your own ball, and then you place it *next to and touching* the ball you've just roqueted, in any position you wish. Then, again hitting only your own ball with your mallet, you send *both balls off in the direction in which you want them both to go.*

At this stage, just absorb that sequence of events, and those two words. Incidentally, this is how to pronounce them:

Roquet: rokay or rókey
Croquet: crokay or crókey
Roqueted: rokayed or rókeyed
Croqueted: crokayed or crókeyed

If you are coming fresh to the game, be encouraged by the fact that if you are going to become good, you are likely to do so fast. But notice that 'if'. A genuine aptitude for croquet usually shows itself quickly, but if you find you're not reducing your handicap as fast as you'd like, don't despair – as long as you're enjoying yourself and travelling hopefully, you'll improve with time. One of the game's current star players, Steve Mulliner, was by no means an overnight success.

The younger you start the better, say the experts, but Patrick Cotter, Bernard Neal, and Lionel Wharrad, all luminaries of the game, came to croquet in middle age. It *is* an advantage, however, to have some experience of another ball game, because that means your eye's already trained.

The one thing you really do have to be is honest. Croquet is unique in that there are no professional players (though Teddy Prentis in Florida earns his living coaching), and individual games, even at tournament level, are not continuously refereed except by the players themselves. What is more, as croquet is a game in which only one player or team at a time plays, it is the player, or striker, who has the responsibility of refereeing. His opponent may not only leave the court, but absent himself entirely while he is not himself playing, since he is not obliged to watch the game, trusting to the integrity of the striker to judge for himself whether he has scored, or committed a fault. If the game were ever to have a professional arm, this custom would have to be replaced by the presence of a permanent referee – something which would be regretted by most players. Incidentally, I hope that – in the absence of a unisex pronoun – lady readers will forgive my using the masculine pronoun to cover both sexes when I'm not writing specifically about women.

Croquet has its fair share of famous players – famous, that is, in other fields, for being an amateur sport, no personality cult has built up around individuals for their playing outside croquet circles. Sir Winston Churchill enjoyed a game, and Sir Compton Mackenzie was President of the Croquet Association for fourteen years. Harpo Marx was so keen on croquet that he kept his mallets in an air-conditioned room, and spent $50,000 on equipment. Averell Harriman had a lawn laid at the United States Embassy in Moscow when he was ambassador there. Sir Michael Tippett and Donald Sinden play. Louis Jourdan used to balance a lit cigarette on the centre peg and then go all around the hoops with both balls before it burnt out. Darryl F Zanuck played, and fellow-player Moss Hart, the playwright and filmwriter, said of him: 'the same qualities that make him a great film producer make him a great croquet player: he never gives up no matter how far behind he is, he trusts no-one but himself, and he hates his opponent with all his heart!'

Of course you needn't take it that seriously, but you'll find yourself getting more out of the game as you improve, because greater possibilities within it will open up to you. And of course then you will want to take it more seriously, and you will become keener on playing to win.

At an advanced level, Croquet is not quite the purely social game some people have taken it to be in the past. Even if you are playing doubles, you will not have time for more than crucial conversation with your partner, and if you're playing singles, you're on your own for the duration of your innings, which may last half-an-hour. But of course it can be a social – or sociable – game, too. One of England's top players, Veronica Carlisle, told me that when she has a friendly game, it is just that: friendly.

> Some people say that croquet players can never have a friendly game, but that's not true. In a "friendly" I will never play a defensive stroke into a corner. I will always shoot at something. I will always try to do things that will push me a long way further forward if they come off, but if they don't, give it all to the opponent . . .

This is the very antithesis of the cowardly 'Aunt Emma' play which I'll tell you about in chapter one, and it follows from it that provided the opponent plays the same way, both sides can have fun, and stretch themselves. I think that no matter how seriously you take a game, you should never lose sight of the fact that you should also enjoy it. And croquet *can* be pure enjoyment, as the following pages will show.

PART ONE

1 BEGINNINGS

'I do not think I know anything of the game of croquet which is worth communicating.' With these somewhat unpromising words one Henry Pollock wrote in the year 1870 to a certain Richard Prior, physician, botanist, Danish scholar, and – more importantly for us – croquet aficionado. However, he then continued to give what little information he did have:

> I first knew the game in Ireland (at the Rectory of Inistioge in the Co. Kilkenny) about twenty-three years ago. It was then a common game, well-known in that part of Ireland, but not played with any great ardour, and I could never get any set of laws from Ireland. I first played the game in England in 1856 or 57. I bought several sets from Mr. Jaques, and he asked me to give him a code of rules, which I did, and he made me an ivory mallet which I then thought and still think is the best material, but too expensive for general introduction, although it will wear for an indefinite period.

In fact, the origin of croquet is still obscure, although it is certain that it was introduced to England from Ireland in about 1850 – albeit in a pretty undeveloped state. However, it achieved popularity so quickly, and to such an extent once it had arrived on the scene, that several early enthusiasts, other than Dr Prior, endeavoured to research it. One such was Arthur Lillie, croquet player and academic writer on the occult elements in Hinduism, and his book, *Croquet: Its History, Rules and Secrets*, also written about 1870, quotes another letter. This was written by the elderly married sister of the Miss Macnaghten (see page 5), who is one of those reputed to have imported the game to England. It is addressed to Lady Antrim, yet another researcher:

> 47 Hertford Street
> Mayfair

> My Dear Lady Antrim,
> All the information I can give you about croquet is that originally it was much played in Northern France, and was introduced by some Irish family to Ireland a long time ago. My brother [sic] wrote out the rules about fifteen or twenty years ago, and gave them to Mr. Spratt, who very quickly spread their fame. Till the rules were written it had been played from tradition, and the mallets made by country carpenters; but the game existed long before my childhood, which is now in the remote ages. I have a vague idea that Mr. James Brownlow knows more about croquet but I am not sure. Is not the change in the weather delightful? How wretched the snow was!

> Ever yours affectionately,
> Octavia Helen Campbell

'Thursday'

Mr Spratt did indeed publish some rules, in 1851, and they are extremely basic, but it was Mrs Campbell's *sister* who gave them to him, not her brother. His setting shows two pegs and ten arches placed seven or eight feet apart in groups making it easy to run up to three hoops in one strike. Spratt describes the course to be followed and then gives the following laconic instructions:

> Players strike their balls alternately: but when a player sends his ball through an arch he is entitled to another stroke, and also when he 'roquets' his adversary, he gets another stroke. 'Roquet' is produced when a player strikes his opponent's ball with his own; he should then put his ball quite close to his opponent's and, placing his foot firmly on his own ball, strike his opponent's ball, and send it as far as possible in an unfavourable direction; his opponent has to play from that point, and his own ball remains steady; then he also gets another stroke.

What Spratt is describing here is the tactic known as 'tight croquet', which is discussed at greater length in chapter two (page 29). He then continues:

> Each player must go through each arch, the proper course, and if he passes an arch he must wait for his next turn.

Dr Prior, in his scholarly and delightful book *Notes on Croquet*, published in 1872, attempts to draw the threads together. Remarking that 'nothing but tobacco smoking has ever spread as quickly' as croquet, he continues:

> I learn from Mr. Spratt of 18, Brook Street, Hanover Square, that more than twenty years ago a Miss Macnaghten brought it to him as a game that had been lately introduced into Ireland, but which she had first seen on the continent in its primitive state – in the South of France, or in Italy, for he forgets which she said – and described as of the simplest and most rustic character. The people of the village chose a hard, knotty piece of wood, bored a hole through it with an auger, and drove a broomstick into it for a mallet. The hoops they made of willow rods. Mr Spratt has still in his possession her letter in which she had drawn up the rules as observed by the peasantry of that country, and will show it to anyone who is curious upon the subject. Mr. Spratt kept the implements in his shop for some years, and, finding no demand for them, sold the game to Mr. Jaques, an enterprising young man who brought it into notice, and no doubt has realized a fortune by it, as he certainly deserved to do.

So far so good, except that when Prior published, Jaques wrote to Arthur Lillie (in 1873):

> I made the implements and published directions (such as they were) before Mr. Spratt introduced the subject to me. The first I made were from patterns which I purchased in Ireland when travelling there on business. Dr. Prior is wrong in assuming that I made a fortune by croquet, though polite of him to think that I deserved to do so.

Nothing can be verified: Spratt's letter from Miss Macnaghten does not survive; Miss Macnaghten, a shadowy figure at the best of times, was burnt to death in a fire (incidentally, a curiously large number of her family met violent deaths – all scrupulously listed by Prichard), and the Hatton Garden factory of John Jaques & Son was burnt to the ground during an air-raid in 1941. The company survived, but all its records and equipment, save for an 1846 pattern book (ie pre-croquet) were destroyed. John Jaques II's great-grandson, the firm's current managing director, tells me that his great-grandfather introduced the game at the Great Exhibition of 1851, and that he was awarded a Gold Medal for his pains. It is certainly fair to say that John Jaques II was the first man to rationalise the rules of the game.

> The history of Croquêt is peculiar [he wrote in the Introduction to his rules], it found its way into the world without any acknowledged parentage, and immediately won a popularity which has almost revolutionized our out-door social life.

He goes on to lament the vast number of varying versions of the game:

> there are hardly two lawns in England where the game is played in the same manner in every respect.

One wonders whether he was a keen player himself, or whether he simply had a tidy mind. I think the latter is more likely: Jaques was a busy man and croquet was not his only concern. And one must accord him a sense of altruism too: he certainly didn't need to regulate the rules of the game to promote sales of croquet equipment – sales were booming despite the lack of any hard-and-fast rules. Some measure of the success of his rules, however, is that they were published virtually annually from 1864–1870 and ran into many tens of thousands of copies. They are recognisably those of the modern game, at least in embryo, and form the basis for later refinement by early avatars of the Croquet Association and by such luminaries of the Victorian croquet scene as Walter Jones Whitmore (see chapter two, pages 14–23).

One significant difference between the early game and the modern one is that originally it was for up to eight players. This was quickly reduced to a maximum of four, and by 1870 singles and doubles were being played much as they are today. The reason was simply that, as only one player can play at a time, the more players you have, the longer the waits between turns, which were according to the colour sequence of the balls – pink, blue, yellow, red, orange, green, black and brown – and the outplayers not surprisingly, became bored.

Looking beyond Miss Macnaghten for an origin to the game, it is tempting to see a link between croquet and pall-mall, a game which has a long ancestry. 'Pall-mall' ultimately derives from the Latin *pila* (a ball) and *malleus* (a mallet). Pall-mall 'malls' and a ball are in the

1   The golf stroke in the game of pall-mall. (*Notes on Croquet*)

possession of the British Museum, but are currently on exhibition at the Museum of London. There are two 'malls' (BM catalogue numbers 1854, 3–6, 1 + 2), and one ball (1854, 3–6, 3), and they are probably the last surviving examples. The game itself can be traced back to Italy and the *Giucator di palea a maglio* mentioned in the carnival songs of Florence by Giovanni dell'Ottonaio, soon after 1500.

In the version which reached England, the method of hitting the ball with the small-headed mallet was exactly like the golf stroke, and

2   A pall-mall court from an eighteenth-century French book, confusingly titled *Jeux d'Allemagne*. (*Mary Evans Picture Library*)

the balls were driven through hoops around a long rectangular course. In all the illustrations I have seen of the game, the hoops are huge – two or three feet high – but, like croquet hoops, firmly planted in the ground. The *Shorter Oxford English Dictionary*, however, has this to say about pall-mall: 'A game in which a boxwood ball was driven through an iron ring suspended at a height in a long alley ...'. Perhaps two versions existed. Either way, by all accounts the objective was to go round in as few strokes as possible.

The surface on which the game was played is also of some interest. Pepys wrote in his *Diary* for 15 May 1663:

> I walked in the park discoursing with the keeper of the Pell-mell, who was sweeping of it, who told me of what the earth is mixed that do floor the mall, and that over all there is cockle-shells powdered and spread to keep it fast.

However, apart from leaving a legacy in London street names, the game itself had disappeared by the mid-eighteenth century and I can find no evidence of a connecting link with croquet which is, in any event, a very different sort of game.

The etymology of 'croquet' and croquet terms is, if anything, even more obscure than the history. However, it might be useful to examine the apparent relationship between 'croquet' and 'cricket', and for this it is worth returning to the redoubtable Dr Prior.

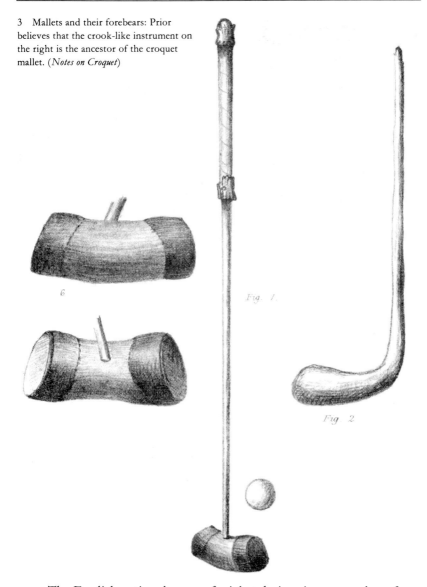

3   Mallets and their forebears: Prior believes that the crook-like instrument on the right is the ancestor of the croquet mallet. (*Notes on Croquet*)

The English national game of cricket derives in name at least from the French *criquet*, which in turn is the diminutive of 'a word retained in all the Germanic languages: Anglo-Saxon *cricc*, Danish *krykke*, Frisian *krik*' – all of which mean a staff, or crutch. In old French *criquet* meant a peg or stump at which a ball was bowled. However, Prior says that he is strongly inclined to suspect that the word originally carried the meaning of 'crook': a crook-shaped bat is the ancestor of many modern mallets, rackets and clubs used in bat-and-ball games, and he quotes many examples and delves deep into etymology to prove his point. Although any directly-linked original word is lost, it seems reasonable to suppose that *croquet* has something to do with *crochet*, a hook, and that the word originally may have been a descriptive noun for the implement used to strike the ball in the lost game which is croquet's ancestor. Alan Ross, a croquet player who was also Professor of Linguistics at Birmingham University, took a different view in the early 1960s, plumping for an Old Erse word, 'cluiche', which means 'play', but the truth of the matter remains tantalisingly unresolved.

Prior has a good deal of fun with the word 'roquet' too: 'Roquet is the diminutive of *roc*, a coat', he begins, and then takes us through Middle Latin, German and Chaucer's translation of *Le Romaunt de la Rose* as well as the original Guillaume de Lorris, together with more erudite and esoteric quotations still, before concluding sternly:

> Without quoting more on the subject, we may say that *rochet*, *roquet*, or *rokette*, has meant, from the earliest occurrence of the word, 'a smock', and let who will, in joke or in earnest, have given it its slang sense of 'hit and go on', we hope that for the future the ladies will forbid the familiar reference to this part of their dress on the croquet-lawn, and insist upon the word being eliminated from the glossary of the game.

Prior continues for another two pages, and gets very worked up:

> ... to use a word that means 'a smock' in the sense of 'hitting a ball', is a case of as pure slang as to call stealing *cabbaging*. It is the wilful misapplication of a word to a subject with which it has nothing to do ... In proof of the uselessness of the word *roquet*, I may state that, to the best of my recollection, in all the hundreds of games in which I have been engaged I have never used it, or been at a loss to express myself without it ... Would that, if employed at all, it had been retained in its proper meaning, and been applied to a disgraceful practice of certain ladies to stand over a ball and conceal it with their clothes, while they scuffle it along with their feet to where they wish it to lie. This might, in strict truth, have been called "roqueting", or "smocking" a ball, but to see the absurdity of the present use, let us only imagine croquet to become fashionable in France, and the ladies, shocked at any allusion to their undress, to replace *roquet* with an English

4   A precise example of crinoline croquet, of the type so much disliked by Dr Prior: the girl is using her skirts to hide a 'cheat'. (*Mary Evans Picture Library*)

term. What if we heard one of them call to her partner, "Petticoatez la boule bleue, ma chère!"

At the end of all this, he suggests the substitution of the word *frap*, from *frapper*, *hit* (rather sensibly, but prosaic after *roquet*), or *roke*, from the Swedish *raaka* – 'which, by a curious accidental coincidence, means "hit"'.

It seems to me much more logical to suppose that roquet comes from a Nordic word for 'hit' than from a Romance word for 'smock', that is if one ignores the tenuous historical connections which croquet has with France and Italy. However, Prior was an etymologist – so perhaps he knows best – and I am not; but that will not prevent me from having some fun also.

There is a croquet expression whose origin is also obscure – the 'Aunt Emma player'. The hallmark of such a player is cowardly tactics (see chapter fifteen, page 152), and indeed an article on 'Cowardly Tactics' appears in Arthur Lillie's book *Croquet Up to Date* under the pseudonym of 'Aunt Emma'. *Croquet Up To Date* was published in 1900, just in time for the Edwardian rebirth of interest in the game, and clearly the expression, even at that early date, was used in its current meaning of a thoroughly irritating player, whose play may be effective but is also selfish, and generally boring for his or her opponent. Lillie gives no explanation of it, and obviously assumes that his readers are familiar with it. No-one in the croquet world knows what the origin of the expression is, but I believe I may have discovered it.

To explain, we must look ahead to the family of Walter Jones Whitmore, who appears in the next chapter and who, in his own extraordinary fashion, did so much for croquet. Walter had an uncle on his mother's side, one Tom Clutton-Brock, who had married a certain Emma Hill, the daughter of a country clergyman. Almost from the beginning she was described as 'Tom's matrimonial blister' by the family, and it was generally assumed (correctly) that she drank. It was observed that whenever she went calling she took a bottle of port with her in the carriage and often refreshed herself from it.

The Whitmore Joneses (it was only Walter who called himself Jones Whitmore), and especially one of the sisters, Mary, very strongly disapproved of Emma, though her letters show her to have been more of a fool than a knave, if also something of a meddlesome bore. The trouble really started when Tom died as a virtual bankrupt. Various family financial complications ensued and there was not enough money to give Emma her proper jointure. The poor woman only had £200 per annum, and out of this she had to keep herself and four young daughters. It was suggested that an annuity should be bought for her, instead of giving her an income out of the estate, and on this subject Mary was bitter:

> I don't like this plan of giving Aunt Emma an annuity – it sacrifices all the children and gives her £300 a year – and subject to *delerium tremens* as she is, her life is not worth six months' purchase, indeed such is her perversity that if she ever became of value she would probably die.

Aunt Emma was a serious thorn in the flesh of the Whitmore Joneses, and although Walter himself is not on record about her, it is fair to assume that he shared his family's dislike of her. From this it's not too fanciful to assume that he used her name in vain as an appropriate appellation for any adversary whose lumbering tactics on the croquet lawn irritated him. Thus Emma Clutton-Brock, née Hill, perhaps lives on, unrecognised until now, on the lips of croquet players throughout the world.

None of this really helps us towards discovering the origins of croquet which, despite all research, still remain enigmatic. Perhaps the last word had better go to the unknown writer – who might have been Prior, or even Lewis Carroll, although that is less likely – of the following poem. It is in mock-heroic style and was printed in *Punch* on 2 July 1864:

Mysterious Croquêt! Like my 'Little Star'
Of Infancy, 'I wonder what you are?'
Owning no parent, yet herein no shame,
Where all the honour would so gladly claim.
May be that, Thou didst give to mortals joy,
When wingèd Time was yet a fledgling boy;
See sporting NIMROD coming from the fields,
Lays down the spear and the gay mallet wields;
A Pre-Noachian Croquêt might have then
Been the delight of Patriarchal men.
As on Assyrian Courtwalls, figure-fraught,
Scholars see something, where the boys mean naught,
So we, upon these walls, (from bias freed),
May the antiquity of Croquêt read.

2 THE VICTORIANS

In 1868 the sporting publisher Horace Cox brought out a thirty-nine-page book called *Croquet Tactics*. It was written by Walter Jones Whitmore and was in its way an important landmark. Walter Jones Whitmore was by no means the first man to write about croquet – *The Field* had indeed published its own croquet laws, as a separate publication, in 1866 – but he may well have been the oddest, and although John Jaques II had done the groundwork, this thirty-seven-year-old member of the Cotswold landed gentry did more than any other single person to create and establish croquet as an organised game. In fact, in a short and fairly desperate life, croquet was his one real triumph.

He was born in 1831, the seventh of ten children, and grew to be considered the clever and good member of the family. Actually it was a fairly mad family, and you cannot blame them when you see the photograph of them, taken in the Great Hall at Chastleton one distant summer afternoon, and now so faded that only the expressions on their faces are unmistakable. Sitting or standing around in an untidy sort of way, they all look rigid with boredom in the dusty sunlight. They were victims of the enforced leisure the Victorian upper-classes suffered, largely but not entirely through their own fault.

Walter did well at school and even went to Oxford for a time, but the first significant event of his life was botching his chances of inheriting the rich Shropshire estate of Dudmaston from his Uncle Wolryche, who had nine daughters but no male heir. The story goes that Walter's arrogant refusal to go and work as his uncle's land-agent cost him the inheritance, but although he certainly *was* arrogant, it's

5   Walter Jones Whitmore. (*Courtesy of Mrs Barbara Clutton-Brock*)

not entirely fair to blame it on that completely in this case. Walter was only seventeen at the time, entertained the strong hope of being called to the Bar after Oxford, and had no interest in or capacity for land-management. He and all his brothers and sisters had loathed the summer holidays at Dudmaston they had been forced to go on as chilren almost as much as they loathed their inflexible and autocratic Uncle Wolryche.

Nevertheless, the loss of the inheritance meant that Walter would have to do something else, and the need to find him something to do became pressing when he failed to pursue his legal career. Walter was a dyed-in-the-wool Victorian romantic: always full of schemes which never came off, either because they were too far-fetched or because he didn't see them through. Fatally, too, he didn't *have* to work. There wasn't much money, but there was enough for him to get by on an allowance – and of course he was firmly in the Victorian gentlemanly tradition of ignoring tradesmen's bills.

A job was found for him in the Treasury and Audit Office. His mother, Dolly, was a great friend of Disraeli's wife, and Disraeli was at the time Chancellor of the Exchequer in Lord Derby's first short-lived government. Disraeli arranged the appointment. Surprisingly, perhaps, Walter took to the Civil Service and earned rapid promotion. He was, however, too high-minded to heed his mother's exhortations to keep in with the Disraelis. He was transferred to the War Office but became disaffected with government work as he became convinced that 'no civil service ever was or ever would be carried on as badly as that of this country' – but he also felt that the senior civil servants were being carried by the juniors, who did all the work. Despite promotion, his arrogance and his butterfly nature prompted him to seek a way out.

Escape came rather unexpectedly in the form of a parlour game which had been invented in 1857 by his otherwise apparently totally useless younger brother, also called Wolryche. The game, called 'Squails', was marketed by none other than Jaques (who didn't only deal in croquet) and enjoyed enormous success. A version of shove-ha'penny crossed with the principle of bowls, it continued to sell well into this century.

> Walter was appointed, or appointed himself, 'London Agent' for the promotion of the game [writes Professor Clutton-Brock], taking a third share of the profits, and since 'Squails' brought in about £200 a year for some years he came to the conclusion that if Wolryche, who was certainly no scholar, could produce so valuable an invention, he himself could produce a much better one and make far more money. And so, since his work in the War Office had made him expert in military matters, he invented 'The Game of War'. Walter was proud of the extreme complexity of the game and repeatedly compared it to chess.

He raised the money to patent the game and have fifty trial sets made from various sources, including £200 from his sister Mary, who was given to writing extremely torrid novels (one still exists in manuscript at Chastleton) but who otherwise appears to be one of the most sensible members of the family. Except, perhaps, in this case.

'The Game of War', marketed by Jaques, was a total flop. 'The public doesn't care to be troubled with a new science', sulked Walter, and at the same time he took a spitefully envious sideswipe at 'Squails',

6   A rare set of Squails. (*From the collection of Christopher Jaques*)

calling it 'the least deserving of games' – though later he was quite unscrupulously to claim that he had invented it himself. One suspects that Walter was one of those people for whom reality and fantasy are merely relative terms.

Bailed out financially by his grudging elder brother, Willie, who had by this time become head of the family, he went on to invent 'The Imperial Chinese Game of Frogs and Toads', which Jaques faithfully put on the market – this time with moderate success. Meanwhile Walter had taken to writing treatises – on every subject under the sun. He wrote in a confident, spiky hand, on sky-blue paper, about everything from the Needle Gun to the 'Great Masters – First Draft: Preface and Synopsis', from dendrology to how to improve the Civil Service. All these papers, neatly bundled and tied with fading red ribbon, together with a mass of unbelievable poetry, lie today damp and mouldering in a wicker flower-basket at Chastleton. Mixed in with them are pieces of plaster and masonry. Some time ago, since Alan Clutton-Brock's death in 1976, penetrating damp at Chastleton caused the ceiling of a room used as a bookstore to collapse, damaging Walter's papers, which have never been salvaged – a sad relic of a vigorous but unfocused intellect. 'The basket's still full of ceiling as well as papers,' says Barbara Clutton-Brock, wistfully.

Walter seems to have had an irrepressible personality:

> He was always ready to teach other people their business, and
> filled up much of his ample leisure by doing so ... He wrote for
> his sister Louisa a long treatise on how to preserve her beauty.
> He told her to apply Atkinson's bear's grease, a pot of which he
> sent her, when to wash her face, and how to brush her teeth with
> two kinds of brush in succession. To retain her superabundance
> of hair she was not to wear a night-cap, 'If it's possible in any
> way to avoid it'.

When his younger brother was still a boy, Walter fidgeted about his
upbringing: 'The fact is,' he admonished his sister Mary, 'that women
have the faintest, slightest notions of what moral discipline consists in'.
Later, Wolryche was to be prevented at all costs from 'sleeping on a
feather bed, from rising late, drinking wine, and sitting on a fender
before the fire'. Walter's opinion was that 'to get up by candlelight
every winter's morning is a more important thing in the education of
a boy than all the rest put together'.

He was responsible for at least sixty inventions, the best of which
are listed by Clutton-Brock, including 'elastic heels for boots', an 'insect
holder', a 'patent croquet stand', and, possibly best of the bunch, a
'bootlace winder', in which 'Walter's soaring imagination achieved its
highest flight'. The device was a reel attached to the top of a boot by
means of which long laces could be drawn up out of the way. A pair
of these winders existed at Chastleton until recently, but are now
unfortunately lost. None of Walter's other inventions survive, and few
got beyond the drawing-board in any case.

He also published two volumes of poetry with Longmans. The
first contains a collection of passable if uninspired work, but the second
is truly dreadful – the result of a misguided attempt to emulate Burns.
Very few copies of either volume were sold, and although the *Morning
Chronicle* referred to the 'exquisite lyrical effusions' of the first volume,
the *Scotsman* said 'it is impossible to do justice to its perfect non-entity
of thought, and irrelevancy of expression'. Clutton-Brock quotes one
or two of the more extraordinary morsels, which Prichard repeats, but I
cannot resist giving you just one more from the vast sheaf of manuscript
poems I have of Walter's: the poem in question is called 'Vaccination
on Parnassus', and supposes the necessity of vaccinating the Muses
against smallpox:

They slanged the Doctor well. The first said: 'Fie, oh!
To go and give such pain to your good Clio!'
'Would then this Doctor my own powers usurp? He
Scratched on my arm the score,' said sore Euterpe.
'Alas! my pastoral shoulders all on fire!
Scratch with my crook – scratch, scratch!' screamed young Thalia,
'I really can't and won't – endure the abomina –
-ble pain,' said with a frown the stern Melpomene.

And so it goes on. The rhymes don't improve, either, with 'chicory/Terpsichore' and 'Pain you/Urania' leading the field. Typically, Walter explains which Muse is which in a margin note.

Turning from poetry, Walter burned briefly with ambition to become manager of the Crystal Palace; and devised a 'foolproof' insurance scheme. Then he wrote a novel, which Longmans actually declined. The family name was Whitmore Jones, but he changed his name to Jones Whitmore because a friend of his named Dickins had persisted in making facetious references to 'Dickins & Jones' whenever they passed the department store in Regent Street.

There was, however, one thing that this curious, contradictory, unstable character did really well, and that was play croquet. And for a man whose other writings were usually intemperate, his *Croquet Tactics* is a model of common sense, insight and intelligence, truly laying the theoretical foundations of the modern game, as we shall see later. The role he played personally in the game's development was somewhat more flamboyant. And yet it was undeniably he who, in Arthur Lillie's words, transformed croquet 'from the silliest open-air game to the most intellectual one'. It is fortunate for croquet that Walter found success with it, for otherwise he would doubtless have quickly dropped it and gone on to the next project his deluded mind told him would make his fortune.

There were two croquet lawns at Chastleton, and they are there still, on the southwest side of the house, now somewhat overgrown. On these Walter was in the habit of playing – chiefly, Lillie says, with ladies. His mind, as is clear from many of his treatises, and from his 'Game of War', was paradoxically (given his behaviour) rather an organised one, and he clearly had a strongly strategic imagination – perfect for a croquet-player. Clutton-Brock describes his first steps towards developing the game, having perceived its potential, and goes on to say:

7   Chastleton House, home of Walter Jones Whitmore.

... in 1867, by a characteristic manoeuvre, he was able to proclaim himself the first of all champions of croquet. He got up a tournament at Evesham, the first open championship ever to be held, though in fact it was not all that open; it was by no means widely advertised or attended, and in consequence Walter won it. Thus he was enabled, as Lillie put it, 'to pose as the champion of croquet', a useful fact in those days.

Unfortunately he could not let well alone but tried to repeat his triumph next year in the second open tournament which he got up at Moreton-in-Marsh (the nearest substantial town to Chastleton). This was well advertised in *The Field* and other newspapers, and attended by many of the best croquet players of the time ... Mark Pattison came to stay at Chastleton and the White Hart at Moreton was crowded with competitors. All the water in the town was used, it was said, to keep the croquet ground green in readiness for the tournament during a dry season. Walter won his first round against G. A. Muntz (a star player), but partly it would seem because Muntz once mistook Walter's ball for his own. In the second round Walter was beaten by W. H. Peel [the same Peel who invented the 'peel' form of play, see page 154], who in due course won the tournament and became champion in Walter's place.

Even so, Walter was a very good and respected player, and he established his position of authority in the croquet world firmly with the publication of *Croquet Tactics*. In it, he recommends the game because, unlike racing and various other sports, it has 'no doubtful set whatever in its train'. This, however, gives an over-optimistic impression of the croquet world then. In looking at the Byzantine and at times internecine atmosphere within croquet politics of the time, it is worth bearing in mind what a wildly popular game it was – remember, too, that it was a potential money-spinner.

Walter was instrumental in helping redraft the *Rules* of the game for *The Field* in 1868, and for this he was allotted half of the profits in the sale of the book. Soon afterwards, he and J H Walsh, editor of *The Field*, formed the All England Croquet Club (1869), which abrogated to itself all authority for the game from this point on, presumably because the AECC had refined the groundwork John Jaques II had done. Walter looked set fair to become The Authority on the game, and he might have succeeded, but for a bitter power struggle that ensued between himself and Walsh, in the course of which each deprived the other of his share of the profits from the rule-book.

> Walter, [says Clutton-Brock], suggested that 'The Field's' rules should be adopted by the AECC so that they might be given more prestige and authority. There was an obvious risk that the AECC might then start altering them, for Walter's ideas about how croquet should be played were by no means shared by all.

He was ahead of his time in preferring narrow hoops, and against the trend in preferring small mallets. Lillie complained that 'he loved a finicking game, and timid, finicking maxims'. But Walter was sure he had enough influence with the AECC to prevent any change. By a rather bald stratagem the AECC committee was to be assigned a share of the profits from the rule-book in return for their support of it – however, the committee was persuaded then to re-assign this share back to Walter!

This might have been fine, but success began to go to Walter's head and he had soon alienated both Walsh and the AECC committee completely. In a series of manoeuvres and counter-manoeuvres, the AECC sought to oust him. And the money that he doubtless dreamed of making from the game was not forthcoming either: up to 1869 only 347 copies of *Croquet Tactics* out of 1000 had been sold, making Walter a grand total of £19. Plenty of mildewed copies are still lying around at Chastleton.

However, Walter still thought he was on to a good thing, and in fairness he must have felt that croquet was his baby, so he dug his heels in: relations between him and the AECC became strained, and then rancorous. Finally the club split, but it is interesting that Walter took with him not only Walter Peel (a younger cousin) but Dr Prior himself. Renamed the National Croquet Club (NCC), Walter's breakaway faction set itself up in rivalry to the AECC, and it found itself a magazine to provide literary counter-blasts to those directed at it by *The Field*. *Land and Water* was edited by Frank Buckland, the first Professor of Geology at Oxford and a noted eccentric (for more on this engaging man, see my *How to be Oxbridge*, Grafton, 1985), and it supported the NCC staunchly until its re-amalgamation with the AECC in 1871.

It was not, in fact, long before the NCC began to falter. It failed to secure a permanent playing-ground – in which the AECC succeeded, at Wimbledon – and it soon began to realise what the AECC had already realised: that Walter, victim as ever of those fatal blemishes in his character which always kept him at one remove from reality, was more of a liability than an asset. He took authority upon himself without reference to the committee. He defied his fellow club-members; he was extravagant with funds; he even misappropriated funds to pay personal expenses, once spending £20 on a vase for himself. In fact, he had only one thing in his favour: he was a gentleman.

It was through his influence that such people as Lord and Lady Essex (who played croquet at their seat at Cassiobury Park in Hertfordshire) and Lord Ilchester had joined the original AECC. Whatever else he didn't have, Walter had class. However, the writing was on the wall, and in order to get rid of him, the members of the NCC had to admit defeat and their mistake, and go back under the wing of the AECC. Walter, still full of fight, then founded the Grand National Croquet Club with a handful of people still loyal to him, which had a brief blaze of glory, culminating in a grand tournament (which also comprised horse-racing and cricket) at Aldershot late in 1871.

Aldershot was Walter's last appearance on the public stage, and he seemingly abandoned croquet to return to Chastleton, to embark on other schemes, other inventions. Perhaps he felt that he'd got all he could out of the game. Certainly by 1872 for the first time his irrepressible optimism seems to have left him, for he writes of 'one long, unaltering, steady series of disappointments'. But he set to work on a

review of all his own inventions; he proposed a scheme to have St
Paul's dome floodlit, 'and any large manufacturer who could do this
might have his name and address in lights on its base'. He was also
working on a book of country house games, 'by the inventor of *Squails,
War, Frogs & Toads, Hard Lines, Mangola*, etc.'. It never saw the light
of day and this was perhaps fortunate, because of course Wolryche had
invented Squails; Hard Lines was invented by his sister, Mary; and
Mangola was the brainchild of a certain Miss Mordaunt.

In June 1872 he went to Jersey, needing a more soothing climate
than that of England because of an infection of the bronchial tubes.
Returning to Chastleton a month later he succumbed to his illness in
the best Victorian tradition and died. He was forty-one. The Grand
National Croquet Club did not survive him. Only his debts did, and,
ultimately, his unique and vital contribution to croquet.

Another odd character – also a writer – was a certain Captain
Mayne Reid. He has to his credit in the British Library at least five full
columns of books of wild adventure of the Tarzan type, but in 1863
he published a book called, simply, *Croquet*. It was revised and reissued
in New York in 1869. The revised edition contained 184 laws, the last
of which read, 'Victory is obtained when all the friends of a side have
struck out. This ends the game, an event usually signalized by a
flourishing of mallets and a triumphant shout of "Victory!".'

Mayne Reid was a flamboyant character of the gentleman-adven-
turer type, but he was also clearly a skilled player with a vision of a
democratised croquet-for-all that we may be coming closer to today:

> though hitherto restricted to the lawn of the lordly mansion and
> confined within the palings of the park, croquet will ere long
> escape from aristocratic keeping and become equally the property
> of the paddock and the village green. Let us hope that no class
> jealousy will arise to prevent its spread.

But Mayne Reid had other fish to fry too, and not the least of these
was to launch a full-scale attack on Jaques. He dismisses Jaques'
equipment as 'quite unsuitable', and goes on to speak of

> the London toymaker [sic] Jaques, who was among the earliest
> manufacturers ... and who by dint of a great deal of advertising,
> gained such a pre-eminence over his trade rivals, that he was
> enabled to set the fashion for all England, and, as we find, also

for America: since the manufacturers in this country [i.e. the USA] appear, one and all, to have copied him to a turn...

Peevishly, Mayne Reid even takes poor Jaques to task for his 'affected' spelling of 'Croquêt'.

The attack continues over pages, quite startling in its savagery:

a ball of boxwood is an absurdity; one of lignum vitae a monstrosity. You may wonder why either should be in use ... the explanation is simple enough, Jaques introduced them, because it enabled him to charge three guineas for a set; while for those of ordinary material [Mayne Reid advocated sycamore, and its American congener, buttonwood] he could only ask a guinea and a half!

At the time Mayne Reid was writing, balls were frequently differentiated by a number of coloured bands painted around them. Jaques sold such balls and attracted this criticism from the choleric Captain:

And this brings us to another of the iniquities introduced by Monsieur [sic] Jaques – the coloured stripe or band around the balls. It was done to avoid concealment of the costly wood! ... anyone should understand that the eye, in making the stroke, must be misled by the stripe.

Jaques had also introduced clips, of corresponding colours to the balls to be affixed to the next hoop a ball had to run.

He even took the trouble, we believe, [says Mayne Reid], to patent them! If you have clips upon your bridges, pluck them off and fling them behind the fence. By doing so you will get rid of a nuisance – with much advantage to your memory.

Mayne Reid's motivation for demolishing Jaques is not far to seek, for he concludes:

Mr. Bangs Williams of 95 William Street, New York, a manufacturer of 'croquet things', has been made acquainted with our ideas, with full instructions for carrying them out; and the result is a set of 'Croqueterie' placed before us, bearing the complimentary title of "Onward", that appear to be correct as to size, shape and playing capacity, besides being more beautiful than any we have ever seen.

He ends with the clear hope of receiving a cut from Mr Bangs Williams 'as the herald who proclaimed them'.

Drawn by DIGAMMA.   Engraved by CHARLES KNAPP & CO.

THE CROQUET QUEEN.
(See Poem.)

8   'The Croquet Queen' – the frontispiece to Captain Mayne Reid's book on croquet.
(Courtesy of the British Library)

The Captain's book includes a five-stanza poem called 'A Warning To Croquetters Against Coquettes'. Here is the first stanza:

You may talk about skating and sleighing and dancing
   Proclaim the delights of the rod and the gun;
Of the ride through the park upon steed gaily prancing;
   The row on the lake until daylight is done;

> Praise the sports of the land, and the water, each one –
> The bath by the beach or the yacht on the sea –
> But of all the sweet pleasures known under the sun,
> A 'good' game of croquet's the sweetest to me.

The frontispiece to his book shows 'The Queen of Croquet', a lady who seems dressed to croquet men by sight rather than by skill.

The captain may, however, have had a point – croquet's arrival filled a gap in the lives of Victorian gentlepersons. One has only to look at the vast, vast variety of parlour games which were invènted and marketed for them to realise that their most constant battle was against the boredom that the enforced leisure of their class condemned them to. These parlour games played their part, but something else was needed: a pastime which provided a forum for young men and women to meet in the open air (the Victorians were great ones for gentle exercise), on equal terms, and which enabled them to put as much distance between themselves and the watchful eyes of their chaperones as possible.

Leech's famous, and at the time frequently reproduced, first cartoon for *Punch* – 'A Nice Game For Two or More' – which appeared on 17 August 1861, sets the tone for a whole run of variations on a theme, a theme taken up by the Music Hall as well. Croquet provided the perfect backdrop for Victorian birds and bees to get busy. It also gave girls a chance to show off clothes to the men, and even, if contemporary prints are anything to go by, risk allowing the glimpse of ankle. No wonder that in the early stages of the game nobody cared much about the rules – an oddity indeed among the order-obsessed Victorians. No wonder that the tradition was born of sending your opponent's ball off behind the rhododendron bushes – and then going with her (or him) to help look for it! And no wonder it was popular – a popularity attested to by the fact that one or two of its technical terms entered the English language permanently as slang (eg: to 'peg out').

This early period of the game came to be known as the era of 'crinoline croquet'. Croquet was treated as a prestige addition to garden parties and often as an opportunity to show off wealth and fashion, 'and even', says Arthur Lillie, 'to flirt, as it must always be remembered that croquet led the way in introducing women on equal terms in sport with men'. Inevitably, young men hoped only that their partners would be pretty, and preferably wealthy, in a period when it was almost inconceivable to expect sporting *skill* from *women*.

A NICE GAME FOR TWO OR MORE.

" —— Fixing her Eyes on his, and placing her pretty little Foot on the Ball, she said, 'Now, then, I am going to Croquet
you!' and Croquet'd he was completely." (*From Rose to Emily.*)

9 The first cartoon about croquet: John Leech's 'Croquet'd he was completely' from *Punch*, 17
August 1861. This picture has been reproduced a thousand times and is still to be seen hanging
in many croquet clubs. (*Punch*)

CROQUÉ'D.

Mamma (severely). "Why are you not Playing with the others, Blanche?"
Blanche (innocently). "Don't know how, Mamma. Major Mallet is Teaching me."

P. H. AYRES' NEW CROQUET ARCHES.

(Patented and Registered.)

As will be seen by the accompanying illustrations the advantage of these new hoops consists in the fact that they cannot sink further into the ground after being properly driven in, the requisite clear space being thus always maintained, while there are no inside projections to cause any deviation in the path of the ball.

All Croquet Sets supplied with these Arches, 1/0 extra.

11 A croquet arch (sometimes called a 'cage') which was used to enliven some versions of the game.

During this period a large number of croquet manufacturing companies sprang up, dominated by Jaques, which is the only one to survive, and the game manifested itself in a variety of forms. There was a large number of different ways of setting the hoops, but the majority of such settings included ten hoops and two pegs. The hoops, which were often called 'arches', were so tall and wide that one of the early players, Arthur Law, had a pet spaniel which he'd trained to run through all of them in order and then touch the winning peg, whenever he set it on the starting point and tapped it with a mallet.

Mallets themselves came in every conceivable shape and size, and the game also was far from standardised. One version even included a 'cage' as well as the two posts. This cage was placed in the middle of the setting and was formed of two hoops crossed, from the centre of which a bell was suspended low enough to be rung by the ball passing through it. The cage became a popular enough innovation to be manufactured and marketed in its own right, though its popularity was relatively short-lived.

> It seems, [says Lillie], to have been confined in England to the Eglinton Castle game of croquet [the home of the son-in-law of the Earl of Essex, who was himself a keen player], and so do the bridges of flat tin called "tunnels" [which at Eglinton replaced hoops]. Lady players were also asked at Eglinton to wear red boots – tight croquet was still played and ladies' ankles were still an unusual sight.

For the sake of accuracy, it should be mentioned that Eglinton Castle is in Ayrshire, in Scotland, not in England. Also, it was only the two side hoops which were replaced by 'tunnels'.

Perhaps the game itself was far less important than the opportunities it provided for other activities, for in the first decade of its life, dating from its official debut at the Great Exhibition, croquet in one form or another had conquered England. You could play it anywhere, on any scrap of lawn, any way you liked; skill didn't matter; and it even seems to have given rise to a minor boom among milliners and bootmakers. The red and gold and blue and silver petticoats described by Disraeli in his novel *Lothair* may also have owed their existence to croquet.

The spread of the game seemed irresistible. It crossed the Channel and was taken up in Europe, and with colonial administrators and soldiers it travelled to almost every part of Britain's then colossal empire. But it was a chaotic plant, growing wildly and unchecked. It needed pruning and cutting into shape, and John Jaques II tried to impose some kind of order by enclosing a copy of his rules with every set he sold. Soon a number of writers had gone into print on the game. Confusion threatened to return, because not all of these writers were in agreement.

It was during this period of anarchy that 'tight croquet' enjoyed its short reign. This is the tactic mentioned very briefly in the previous chapter in the extract from Mr Spratt's rules (see page 4). However, it perhaps deserves a little more comment.

There are innumerable Victorian and Edwardian drawings and cartoons of the game, depicting the tight croquet stroke. They frequently show an elegant and upright gentleman, foot firmly and smugly on one ball (his own) – as though it were so much dead tiger – while preparing to send the other ball (and his opponent) 'off into the rhododendrons'. To the uninitiated, who has nonetheless seen the cartoons or heard of the tactic, it has seemed so unpleasant – to say nothing of the character of the player who employs it – that the reputation of croquet itself has suffered. In fact, this is a double misapprehension.

For a start, the tactic was only in vogue for a very short period of time. (It is not even permitted in the modern version of the game.) Secondly, even when it was in vogue, it was more of a prohibition against moving one's own ball than a licence to devastate one's opponent's position. In 1864, John Jaques II, wrote in his *Croquêt, the Laws and Regulations of the Game*, in reference to some preceding old laws which he was politely demolishing:

> The allowing or forbidding a player to move his own ball when he takes Croquêt: The first-published rules *did not allow a player to*

12   Tight croquet – from John Jaques' II *Croquet*, 1864.

move his ball. If he did so, he was obliged to leave it in its new position, or replace it, at the option of the opposite side. This law was soon varied, and a note was generally added to the old rule, as follows:– "A player, in Croque'ing a ball, may place his foot lightly on his own ball, and move it with the same blow with which he moves the other ball". In the following rules I have favoured the innovation, because in what are termed "following strokes" and "splitting strokes", great skill and beauty of play are shown, which are entirely lost in "Tight Croquêt".

'Following strokes' (although no longer called by this term) and 'splitting strokes' are also described in chapter fourteen, pages 135–138, and they do indeed require skill. John Jaques II continues:

When a player strikes his own ball so that it follows the ball he is Croque'ing, he is said to make a "following stroke" and when he strikes it so that it takes a different direction to the Croque'd ball, he is said to make a "splitting stroke". Anyone who has once learned to make these strokes skilfully will certainly never be contented to revert to the old style of "Tight Croquêt", there being so much more "play" in the new method; and as skilful players will, no doubt, finally carry the day, it is possible that in some years "Tight Croquêt" will become altogether obsolete.

John Jaques II, writing when the game was only thirteen years old, clearly saw what we all see now, that in the croquet stroke your own ball and the croqueted ball should *both* be sent to positions of advantage to you. There is no point at all in sending your opponent off (under the modern laws your turn would end if you did so). However, for a while, with John Jaques' revision of the Laws, the tactic became optional: '... it is not obligatory to put the foot on [the ball] at all. This is entirely at the option of the player'. And, as he had predicted, the tactic eventually died.

Meanwhile, by the early 1860s croquet was attracting some heavy guns: Lewis Carroll and Mark Pattison were playing at Oxford (Pattison is even reputed to have turned down the Vice-Chancellorship because it would have interfered with his croquet, though alas the story is apocryphal: Pattison himself writes, in his cold way: 'When the Vice-Chancellorship came to me I had the moral courage to refuse it; and I am fairly entitled to say that since the year 1851 I have lived wholly for study') – and Carroll cheerfully immortalised the game as it was played in the early days in *Alice's Adventures Under Ground*.

Dunbar Isidore Heath, the Egyptologist and Rosetta Stone expert, and his son James, were both keen players, and James Heath's *The Complete Croquet Player* (1875) is one of the best early works on the game. J T C Ross, India's Surgeon-General, and the Viceroy himself, were both players, and J H Walsh had been an eminent eye surgeon before taking on the editorship of *The Field*, the sporting magazine which carried croquet throughout its Victorian heyday. Dr Prior, whom we have met, was a physician, a distinguished and world-travelled botanist and a translator of ancient Danish ballads. Under the influence of these men and others croquet grew into a sophisticated, disciplined and skilful game.

3 THE OUTPOSTS OF EMPIRE

AND BEYOND

So phenomenal had been croquet's success once it had taken hold that it is not surprising that the game immediately spread beyond the narrow confines of England. Young men were travelling to all points of the compass as soldiers, civil servants, administrators or businessmen, and they took their favourite game to wherever the map was coloured pink.

In India it was played by no less a personage than the Viceroy himself, Sir John Lawrence. He is reported to have had an ivory mallet – perhaps part of one of Jaques' luxury sets of the period: 'containing set of $3\frac{5}{8}''$ BOXWOOD BALLS, set of solid IVORY MALLETS, Hoops, Patent Clips, &c, &c'. This set, retailing at £20 in the late 1860s, was at the very top of Jaques' range. Croquet became quite a craze in India, and Arthur Lillie writes that among the English ruling elite 'satraps governing tracts of country larger than Germany were as anxious about their turf as they were about their territories'.

The Surgeon-General, J T C Ross, recalled playing in hilly Simla, which must have been an odd experience, for the croquet courts were small and mainly gravel surfaced because of the poor grass – a fact which might seem astonishing to anyone who looks at the lush lawns of Government House today. 'Croquet reached India in the hot summer of 1864,' believed Ross. '... Hoops were large, with rounded tops, but balls about the weight and size now used.' (In croquet's early days weight of balls, and width of hoops went through almost as many variations as the size and shape of mallets until standardised. Even today, some so-called 'croquet' sets offer nothing like the correct equipment.)

HOW WE PLAY CROQUET AT BUDDLEAPOOR!

13   A *Punch* cartoon of the 1860s.

The game was played right across India, from Peshawar to Calcutta. At Calcutta the courts were all grass, of lovely turf, and naturally very level. Sets were imported from England, and Jaques equipment on the whole preferred, although mallets came to be produced locally – using Simla mountain ash for the shafts, and lignum vitae or wild box for the heads.

Rules seem to have been pretty generalised. Two of Arthur Lillie's Indian croquet-playing informants, a certain General Lane and a certain Mrs Davidson, have this to say: 'There were hoops a child could crawl through', remembers Lane; and Mrs Davidson:

> All through one of our tours in Bundelkund (in central India) we sent on an army of coolies to prepare the ground in time for our arrival at different villages

and she also refers to candle-lit croquet, with candles stuck into each hoop to enable play to continue after dark – something which croquet-players still do at 'garden' level of play. 'Agra was a centre of good play', she says, but adds that Bombay hardly played at all.

14   HH The Maharajah Gaekwar of Baroda playing croquet in front of his palace. From the
Croquet Gazette of 6 May 1909. (*Courtesy of the Croquet Association*)

Croquet in India seems to have lapsed with the advent of lawn tennis (see chapter five), and with the withdrawal of the British, something which is borne out by the fact that Jaques has no record of sending sets to India since the blitz of 1941 destroyed the company's papers; but a photograph in the *Croquet Gazette*, for 6 May 1909, shows 'H.H. The Maharajah Gaekwar of Baroda' playing croquet in front of a vast wedding-cake of a palace. This must have been part of the Edwardian revival of croquet, for Ross writes:

> in the Seventies the game seems to have dropped a good deal, for moving about in many parts of India, I found badminton and lawn tennis were the prevailing games. Only at one station in the wilds of Assam did I find the game in full swing in 1875.

One present-day Far Eastern croquet player is Paduka Seri Begawan Sultan General Sir Omar Ali Saifuddien, the father of the Sultan of Brunei.

Croquet also invaded Africa – or at least those parts of it that fell under British influence. One acquaintance of mine remembers playing it there for the first time and getting hooked. The croquet lawn was on a steep slope and the 'peg' was a twenty-foot-high anthill in the middle! He remembers having a marvellous *alfresco* lunch beforehand, and cooling off in the nearby swimming pool in between turns. It is always, incidentally, a good idea to have a swimming pool close to your croquet lawn when playing in a hot country. The Zambian lawns had good grass, he remembers, but then there were always plenty of staff available to keep them watered.

With the decay of Empire in Africa, croquet faded too. But South Africa is still one of the major croquet-playing countries. The game has been played there since 1860, and the South African Croquet Association, founded in 1936, has always been affiliated with the British Croquet Association. Most of their clubs today are around Cape Town, where the climate is Mediterranean, and Natal, where it is sub-tropical. All courts are now grass, though there used to be clay courts too. The South Africans play to International Laws, with occasional forays into American Rules. In 1982, in fact, the South Africans beat the Americans in that year's International Challenge Cup Tournament in Florida. Jaques equipment is used, and membership of the Association is open to all races, colours and creeds, without exception. Also in Africa, until very recently, croquet has been played in the Gezira Club in Cairo, whose lawns are among the best in the world.

Outside Great Britain and the Republic of Ireland, croquet is not played much in Europe. There are a couple of clubs in Sweden, one in Switzerland, and two in Spain. The first of these, in Jerez de la Frontera, was founded in 1979 by Enrique de Bobadilla and his wife, Angeles Diéz. It has sixteen playing members, and is open 'all year round to any and all croquet-loving players'. It operates, says Enrique in a letter to the author, on the principle of 'no dues, no don'ts'. In winter old Oloroso or Amontillado is served, and in summer, ice-cold Fino, though gin and tonic is also on tap.

Play is taken very seriously, despite the generous hospitality. Richard Rothwell and Robin Godby were invited to go there at the new club's expense to teach the members proper croquet. Richard remembers a beautiful lawn of imported American grass seed (Kentucky Blue Bent grass), on what had originally been laid as a bowling green. Because of the heat, play starts at six pm and continues, floodlit, until one or two in the morning. As in Zambia, one spends one's outplayer periods in the swimming pool.

In Germany, croquet is virtually unknown, though there was a Forces club, started by Rothwell near Paderborn, just after the war. In France, the real game is played by a select few of the very rich. Ordinary mortals play a kind of backyard version which has no great relationship to Association Croquet.

Croquet is played in Russia, and the Croquet Association even has one member there – though he is a diplomat in the British Embassy. There are a number of private croquet courts in the USSR, and the game is followed enthusiastically, although it is played with old-fashioned, wide hoops and large, cumbersome mallets.

Elsewhere in the world croquet is played in the West Indies, Canada and Singapore, although outside Great Britain the two major croquet-playing nations are Australia and New Zealand. The United States would also form part of this group, but a so-far insurmountable difficulty lies in the differences between the US Rules and the International Laws of the game. As it is, only the Santa Barbara Croquet Club plays International Laws, and Jack Osborn, the US Croquet Association President, is a jealous guardian of USCA Rules. Some compromise should be worked out, however, as it would be to everybody's advantage to bring the USA into the one major croquet International – the MacRobertson Shield (see chapter six, page 54 and Appendix D).

The most exciting recent newcomer to the game is Japan, where croquet is catching on very fast, and where jaques already has a contract to sell equipment – a sure sign that the Japanese are taking it seriously! Japan also has its own unsophisticated form of croquet – 'gate ball', which over twenty years has attracted a following of two million players. Croquet itself has been going in Japan since 1983 but already receives modest television coverage – something which the Americans and the British are very eager to get too; and croquet in Japan isn't without the odd dramatic incident, either: recently a wild boar, fleeing from a hunter, crashed into a croquet court in Okayama. It injured four of the elderly players before the others beat it off with their mallets.

Jaques is not unduly worried that the Japanese will just buy a handful of sets and then start copying them themselves, because a croquet set, if it is worth anything at all, cannot be mass-produced – too much hand-finishing is involved. In 1983 Japan invited Bernard Neal over to show them International Laws croquet, and Teddy Prentis to show them USCA Rules. So far they have shown a tendency to prefer the International Rules.

There are signs that croquet is being taken up in China, too, though croquet is nothing new to the Chinese. A picture from the *Illustrated London News* of 1938 shows a Revolutionary Guard about to make a roquet!

Returning to Great Britain, the Scottish Croquet Association was

15   The most unusual croquet player ever? A Chinese communist guerilla prepares a rush. From *The Illustrated London News*, 2 April 1938.

founded in 1973, and is thriving; Wales and Northern Ireland have yet to come to the fore, though each country is represented in the game by individual players. All in all, at home and abroad, croquet is enjoying a renaissance the like of which has not been seen since the Edwardian revival.

4 TRANSATLANTIC CROQUET

Asked to describe the Croquet God – the unseen deity who controls the game from above, one veteran American player said: 'He has the aggression of a man and the vindictiveness of a woman.'

This might be taken as a measure of the grim determination with which the game is approached in the States. However, this has not always been the case. In the early days, and the perhaps not-so-early days, the game still apparently retained some of its original frivolity. For, although croquet had travelled successfully elsewhere and even been played by eminently respectable British in India, in North America in the 1880s critics and moralists perceived a surprising danger in the game, which had not been noticed elsewhere. Indeed, in Boston it was banned, because it was deemed that the sight of so much female ankle was bad for the young men's blood pressure. In 1898 the game was even described by one journal as 'the gaping jaws of Hades' – which seems a little extreme.

Another thing about croquet which upset the Americans was that people bet on it.

Enthusiasts brushed such objections aside, and the game flourished. Unfortunately it nosedived rather when at the end of the nineteenth century the British Croquet Association decreed that mallet heads should be made entirely of wood, the only other material allowed being brass bindings. The Americans, who had been playing with mallets variously rubber- and metal-ended (also allowed in Britain up until 1900) objected to this, and their National Croquet Association symbolically dropped the 'c' at the beginning of 'croquet' and the 't'

16   An etching by Winslow Homer, 1869: 'Summer in the Country'. It originally appeared in *Appleton's Journal of Popular Literature, Science and Art*, and is now in the collection of the Bowdoin College Museum of Art. (*Mary Evans Picture Library*)

at the end of it, and developed their own game of 'roque'. Played on clay courts surrounded by low concrete boundary walls, with nine side 'wickets' ('hoops' in nearly all other countries) it was introduced at the 1904 Olympics at St Louis, Jack Osborn, President of the US Croquet Association, writes in his book on the game. He doesn't say what countries participated, but it may have been a purely US interstate event.

Though the game flourished right through the Depression, it has now all but disappeared. Jack Osborn believes that the American Roque League may still have a headquarters in North Carolina, and he tells me that there is a Kentucky Croquet Association that *thinks* it's playing croquet but is in fact playing roque.

Roque gave birth to variants of its own and generally muddied the American scene for many decades. In the thirties, the true game was kept alive by a handful of people in a handful of clubs, and by a group of intellectuals and artists in Hollywood on the one hand, and among the Round Table group at the Algonquin Hotel in New York on the other. The New York croquet-players, who met at Herbert

Bayard Swope's Long Island estate, included George S Kaufman and Dorothy Parker, as well as Alexander Woollcott and Averell Harriman. Croquet on the west coast centred on the lawns owned by Darryl F Zanuck and Samuel Goldwyn. As Moss Hart once said, 'Sam was formidable because he had a shot called "Sam's crush" – a way of pushing the ball through a wicket. No-one complained. It was his court.'

Since the mid-1970s, croquet in the USA has experienced an astonishing revival, which is due to the work of one man – Jack Osborn. He has pushed the game so successfully that in its first ten years the US Croquet Association (founded in 1977) developed from five clubs to 250, and from a few hundred members to over four thousand.

Croquet is now the second fastest-growing game in the USA, after windsurfing. Centred on Palm Beach, it remains for the moment in the domain of the rich, although as more and more schools and universities are taking it up, there are signs that it will become increasingly democratised. The smallest club, The Round Island Mallet Club in Greenwich, Connecticut, New York, comprises only one family; the Alaska Croquet Club, based in Anchorage, must be the northernmost club in the world; and one of America's foremost players, who also makes his own mallets, is Archie Burchfield, a tobacco farmer, from Stamping Ground, Kentucky.

The USCA's two sister organisations, Croquet International and The Croquet Foundation of America, handle marketing and fundraising respectively. A number of instruction videotapes have been made, featuring such masters of the game as Nigel Aspinall (one of several 'foreigners' who play in America regularly).

The American season is highlighted by two major events: The International Croquet Ball, at which the men traditionally wear black tie but white sneakers, to coincide with the National Club Team Championships in April, and the US Croquet Hall of Fame Ball in September, which is linked to the National Singles and Doubles Championships. Funds raised from these events are ploughed back into teaching the game.

Spectators are being 'educated' too, by means of loudspeaker commentary at tournaments to explain what's going on – if you don't know what's happening there's no point in watching. Whether the commentary is distracting to players, I don't know. Keith Wylie has suggested to me his own idea of providing a commentary via wire-less

17 Jack Osborn, Roehampton, 1985, explaining how the ball just trickled through hoop four to end up in a very awkward position. (*P L Alvey*)

earphones, such as are used for simultaneous translation of foreign-language plays in the theatre. The only problem with that would be the expense.

Croquet in America is enjoying a boom, and more and more people want to learn how to play it. Its appeal at present is particularly to 'young, upwardly-mobile professionals', and it's been described as 'a very up fad', with the proviso that it hasn't perhaps yet 'achieved critical mass'. Its attractions for the young businessman are that it is very smart, that it is centred on an 'upscale' social group, and that you can become proficient at it very quickly. In the States, advertisers of products directed at the rich and at 'achievers' are encouraged to use croquet as their vehicle, and many, such as Rolex watches, do. Golf and country clubs, and good hotels, are installing croquet courts. Shipping lines have even organised croquet cruises. And although Jaques' equipment is widely sold, domestic manufacturers like Forster and Skowhegan are beginning to enter the market too. Perhaps that proviso about achieving critical mass is already out of date.

One hears a lot about the snobbery associated with croquet, although nowadays, in England, croquet on a public level is quite a municipal game, and if current trends continue, it will become as classless as bowls. Nonetheless, perhaps the English connection is partly the source of the snobbery which is much more prevalent in America – certainly as far as croquet in Palm Beach is concerned. And Palm Beach is important, for it is the new headquarters of the USCA.

Not that it's as simple as that. There are two Palm Beaches – the Thing Itself, a fortress of Old Money on the shores of Lake Worth, home of the Breakers Hotel; and West Palm – home of the Palm Beach Polo & Country Club, where the USCA National Club Team Championships take place in the Spring. The social differences between the two Palm Beaches are important: Palm is Establishment, West Palm is Yuppie. Palm has the lowest crime rate in the USA, but enjoys about four times the policing of the national average. Jogging shirtless is frowned on, and the dustmen collect five times a week. West Palm has mosquitoes, but it also has pzazz, hi-tech, and Louis Vuitton sidewalks. It is also socially mobile and relatively open. An American television camera scanning the watchers at a croquet match there, however, still drew the comment from the reporter that 'it looks like the only thing that would upset this lot would be a Democratic landslide'. Fundraising events get Famous Faces to wield a mallet now and then, or treat you to the non-playing appearance of Zsa Zsa Gabor, complete with her lookalike mother and dog.

But there's also a new wave of players. Bill and Becky Hoy, from Atlanta, graduated from the 'backyard' version of the game – and helped launch the Original Invitational Cosmic Croquet and Fantasmajoric Boogie in 1975 in a Georgia cornfield. It's a three-day costume party and tournament for a hundred players, and it's always scheduled to coincide with the full moon. 'If you will be offended by anything,' warn the invitations, 'please don't come.'

The Hoys now run the Georgia Croquet Club, which they founded in 1982, and Bill makes mallets. He says, 'It's not important who you are, or even how you play the game. What's important is your love of croquet.' This is a good attitude, a world away from the glacial exclusivity of the silk blazer brigade at the Palm Beach Bath and Tennis Club, for example; and it's good for croquet in America that it's taken root in *West* Palm. Although it's 'upscale' at the moment, as more and more people come to realise that croquet is fun, and that you don't have to be a Pulitzer to play it, there's little doubt that it will filter through to a wider public in the best way possible – naturally.

5 SPHAIRISTIKE AND
RESURRECTION

With the acquisition of the Wimbledon ground, and the death of the volatile Walter Jones Whitmore, croquet entered a period of relative stability and calm, secure in its position of outmatching and outclassing any other ball game. The laws had been regularised, and the equipment to a great extent standardised, as had the proportions of the lawn, the type of setting, and the number of hoops. By 1872, there were two pegs (one in the centre at either end of the laws) and six hoops (the 'Hale' setting, which survived until 1922). But no sooner had croquet achieved a zenith of popularity than it began to fall from favour. Perhaps the enthusiasts had over-regulated it, and taken the fun out of it for most people.

Dr Prior, writing as early as 1872, realised that there was a problem and sought to identify it.

> To many it will, and I know that it does appear of very trifling consequence, in what posture a player stands as he strikes his ball, so that the stroke is well directed and with the proper strength. But to the outside world, to those who know nothing of the game, but might be tempted to take it up if it were presented to them in an attractive form, this is a matter of the very first consideration. We hear from day to day, and from every part of the kingdom, that ladies are abandoning croquet and arming themselves with bows and arrows again. This may be partly due to the present size of lawns requiring a strength that not all women possess, *and partly to more attention being required in the present advanced*

state of the game than they are willing to bestow it, but is, I am convinced, in a much greater degree than they will avow, due to the attitudes that they see assumed in order to swing the ponderous mallets that are now in fashion – attitudes that they do not admire and are not at all desirous to imitate. In a word, croquet is come to be thought an unbecoming game compared with archery. It is possible that the reluctance of good players to combine with a partner of inferior strength at croquet parties, *or to make their appearance at them at all, may also diminish the interest and pleasure taken in the game in its earlier days* ... It is of no use to blink our eyes at the truth. Croquet is going out of fashion. [My italics]

Dr Prior goes on to suggest ways of relaxing the game – the reintroduction of slightly wider hoops, the reduction of the lawn size, and so on. The main point is that croquet had become too scientific and too abstruse to be attractive, a lesson which evangelists of the game are having to relearn today in their presentation of croquet to the uninitiated – for no game seems to be the object of greater prejudice.

As things stood in 1872, Prior's prophetic gloom proved accurate: after the gorgeous, popular anarchy of the game in the 1850s and '60s, the developed, scientific game of the 1870s was riding for a fall.

In 1874 a new game was introduced to the market in a smart boxed set. One is still to be seen at the Wimbledon Lawn Tennis Museum. It was accompanied by a tiny pamphlet of only eight pages, published by Harrison & Sons of 59, Pall Mall, which described the new game and gave its rules. The title page reads:

Σφαιριστικὴ
The Major's Game of Lawn Tennis
dedicated to The Party Assembled
at Nantclwyd in December 1873
        by WCW

WCW was Walter Clopton Wingfield, a youngish ex-army officer who had turned inventor of parlour games, toys, and, well, inventions in general. His game was based on Real Tennis, and in his preface he explains its history, providing it with a delightfully spurious ancestry:

The game of Tennis may be traced back to the days of ancient Greeks under the name of σφαιριστικὴ ... it has only now died out owing to the difficulties of the game, and the expense of erecting courts. All these difficulties have now been surmounted

18 The cuckoo in the nest – an advertisement from the 1870s for Walter Wingfield's game of Lawn Tennis, or 'Sphairistike'. (*Courtesy of the Kenneth Ritchie Wimbledon Library*)

by the inventor of 'Lawn Tennis', which has all the interest of 'Tennis', and has the advantage that it may be played in the open air in any weather by people of any age and of both sexes. In a hard frost the nets may be erected on the ice, and the players being equipped with skates, the Game assumes a new feature, and gives an opening for the exhibition of much grace and science.

Croquet, which of late years has monopolized the attention of the public, lacks the healthy and manly excitement of 'Lawn Tennis'. Moreover, this game has the advantage that, while an adept at Tennis or Raquets would speedily become a really scientific player, the merest tyro can learn it in five minutes sufficiently well for all practical purposes.

Thus the astute and market-conscious Major Wingfield concludes, cutting an impatient swathe through all the pedantry of croquet – an attitude which people sympathised with in vast numbers, for within a year, 'Sticky' as it briefly became known, had swept the country, finding especial favour with the young. Its six rules, recognisably for the same game as is played today, comprise barely a hundred words and cover two sides of a page. At roughly the same time, croquet had thirty-six laws covering sixteen pages.

Lawn tennis ought to have made Wingfield a rich man, but unfortunately he could not claim to have invented, and therefore claim copyright on, the idea of tennis upon which his game was based. Rival manufacturers quickly grew up, and Wingfield himself dwindled to obscurity in the shadow of his invention. Even so it was merciful that Walter Jones Whitmore had died two years earlier, for one can imagine the agonies of envy he would have gone through if he'd still been alive.

By early 1875 one croquet lawn at Wimbledon had been set aside for lawn tennis. Just over two years later the name of the AECC was changed to The All England Croquet and Lawn Tennis Club. In the same year, 1877, the first lawn tennis championships were held.

From now on lawn tennis began to push croquet into the wings. J H Hale, inventor of the Hale setting (see page 126), and of the bisque (see page 153), said that he had put forward the idea of lawn tennis at the same time as Wingfield, and many other former supporters of croquet, including J H Walsh and Henry 'Cavendish' Jones, turned to the new game. Jones even went so far as to be instrumental, in 1882, in getting the very word 'croquet' taken out of the club's title, so that it became, simply, 'The All England Lawn Tennis Club'. Former followers of croquet now turned against it with Janissary-like zeal: the very boards in the pavilion inscribed with the names of past croquet champions were ordered to be taken down and 'thrown into the Thames'. Fortunately they were preserved by a groundsman and one, at least, which bears the name of the last Victorian champion, A H E Spong, is on show in the Lawn Tennis Museum at Wimbledon.

Croquet was ousted, both from Wimbledon and from its position of unrivalled popularity, but it was not dead. It moved, if you like, underground, to the provinces and the home counties, and its flame was kept alive by players who remained sturdily loyal – not the least of whom was Dr Prior. Under the new name of the United All England Croquet Association, tournaments were organised around the country, even reappearing modestly at Wimbledon. By May 1897 Mr Slazenger's sporting journal *Lawn Tennis* had changed its name to *Lawn Tennis and Croquet* (though croquet was rather a poor relation in the magazine), and by November 1899 the Wimbledon Club changed its name again – to The All England Lawn Tennis and Croquet Club – a title it still has, although early papers bearing the name have the words 'and croquet' printed very small indeed. Added to which, Wimbledon today only has one croquet court. It is not full-size. And you may not join the club purely as a croquet-playing member any more.

In 1900 the present Croquet Association was born, and 1904 saw the first edition of the *Croquet Gazette*. A new headquarters had been found at Roehampton, and a new generation of players was growing up who had only learnt the 'proper' game. Crinoline croquet was just a memory and croquet itself was ready to come in from the cold.

Despite the occasional ruction within its government, the Croquet Association increased its membership from 200 to 2,300 between 1897 and 1914. The period also saw an influx of players from Ireland, among whom the best remembered today are probably Cyril Corbally and Duff Mathews. What they brought with them was the centre-stance. Nowadays, this stance is effectively the only one seen, but the Victorians had all used the side-stance. Women, of course, could not use the centre-stance until much later, when skirts became shorter and looser, or when it became permissible to play in slacks, or even shorts. The first woman to adopt the centre stance (or Irish stance as it was then called) was Mrs Longman, who was playing it in 1936 when Richard Rothwell first came to the game. He remembers that she had specially tailored skirts made to allow for centre-stance play with ease and decorum. The Irish swept the board in tournaments and brought a

THE OFFICIAL ORGAN OF THE CROQUET ASSOCIATION.

No. I. Vol. 1. Wednesday, April 27th, 1904. Price 3d.

JAQUES' CROQUET.

ASSOCIATION BOXWOOD BALLS.

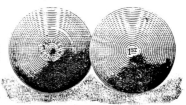

Guaranteed correct size and weight, without being loaded or plugged, and made from the finest Turkish Boxwood. No Persian or other inferior growth of wood box is used, and any 1st quality ball proving defective will be exchanged. A large stock ready for immediate delivery.

1st Selected Match Quality in wood box, **12s. 6d.** per set.
2nd Quality (unstamped) . . . . **10s. 6d.** ,,

Sets may be had with balls weighing 15, 15¼, 16 or 16½oz. as desired.
The 1st quality balls are stamped "1st, Jaques, London," or they are not genuine, and our guarantee does not hold good.

THE ASSOCIATION MALLET

With boxwood head and hickory shaft.

PRICES.

The Weights are only approximate.

1A.—Head, 8in. by 3in., 2lbs. 12oz. .. **8/-**
2A.— ,, 8½in. by 3in., 2lbs. 14oz. .. **8/6**
2B.— ,, 9¼in. by 2¾in., 3lbs. 2oz. .. **9/-**
3A.— ,, 9in. by 3in. 3lbs. 2oz. .. **9/**

EXTRAS.—Gold Cape leather-bound Handl **1/-** ; Cork covered Handle, **1/-**
To special dimensions or weigh not tested, **1/-** ; New Thumb Rest, **1/-**.

The boxwood used for the heads has been specially imported for the purpose, and is free from knots and cracks. The shafts are of special shape and fitted with a cane splice. The handles are octagon shape, and bound with suitable cord. This pattern of mallet is the most popular that has ever been devised.

FIG. 1. FIG. 2.

THE ROEHAMPTON HOOPS AND SOCKETS

(FIG. 1.) ☞ AS USED AT THE RANELAGH CLUB.

The hoops can be removed and replaced without lifting the sockets for rolling or mowing.
For rigidity and accuracy these hoops have no equal.

Price, Hoops, Sockets, Drills, Hammer and Gauge in box complete, **£1 1s. 0d.**

Iron Plugs to place in Sockets when Hoops are removed for any length of time, 1s. 6d. per set of 12.

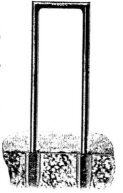

THE ASSOCIATION HOOP

(FIG. 2.)

This is a more permanent pattern. The shape of the bases is such that the hoops stand throughout the season in an upright position, and retain their rigidity without being touched.

19 The cover of the first *Croquet Gazette*, 27 April 1904. (*Courtesy of the Croquet Association*)

20   Miss Lily Gower. Photo by J. Mathias used as the frontispiece for Arthur Lillie's *Croquet up to Date*, 1900.

breath of fresh air into English croquet.

Another innovation, which however did not really catch on until the 1960s, and which is still only seen with any frequency among serious players, was the square-headed mallet. In his *Croquet Up To Date*, published in 1900, Arthur Lillie remembers receiving at one tournament 'fearful news at high tea concerning the play of a certain Mr. M ... hailing from Midlothian, who, they say, never misses anything at all, and plays with a square, brass-headed mallet'. This is the earliest reference to a square mallet that I can find.

The turn of the century also saw the arrival of the first great woman player. Lilias (or Lily) Gower really dominated the game during the Edwardian era, and hot on her heels came Dorothy Dyne Steel, who was always known as 'DD'. DD was at her peak between the wars, but continued to play even after 1945. Among the Englishmen who were making a contribution at this time, C D Locock and Lord Tollemache were most prominent.

Locock was a scholar of Norse languages, and a croquet player of great skill. His book, *Modern Croquet Tactics*, published in 1907, is still regarded as one of the best there is on the game. Lord Tollemache's *Croquet*, which appeared in 1914, is full of photographs of himself demonstrating the various shots and strokes, and came complete with a useful pull-out plan of a croquet lawn. Throughout this period, people were busy polishing and refining the game, and in almost every respect it resembled the game as it is played today. Evolution had been quick – in the Victorian era it had still been possible to use the shaft of your mallet like a billiard cue for certain strokes, and the mallet came supplied with a padded leather end to its shaft for the purpose!

That croquet was enjoying renewed popularity was reflected in the large number of manufacturers of equipment – Piggott's, and Benetfink's, Prossor's and Ayres – and in the large number of spin-off games that abounded: 'Maltese Cross Croquet', 'Kingball', 'Doxil', and

21   An Edwardian advertisement for Table Croquet, including a guarded 'plug' from Lilias Gower. (*Courtesy of the Croquet Association*)

22   Cartoon of Dorothy Dyne Steel by H F Crowther-Smith from his 1929 book, *Croquet Nonsense*

'Cozzare' all feature in an Ayres catalogue as early as 1886; of 'Cozzare' it is said that it 'possesses all the best features of croquet but unlike that Game and Tennis, requires NO SPECIAL SHAPE, OR SIZE OF LAWN'. Table croquet, introduced in Victorian times, and usually played on a billiard table, was revived, and finally Jaques' catalogue for 1910 shows a great variety of mallets, hoops and balls, as well as croquet ball carriers, croquet stands, mallet-cases and holdalls, bisque recorders, ball-repairing compendiums, and even a patent 'croquet target' for practising shots between turns. None of these last are still marketed by Jaques, but Jack Osborn refers to Louis Vuitton mallet cases as being desirable optional extra for jetsetting croquetomanes in America!

Meanwhile a certain amount of bickering continued. One little row, which started before the First World War and was not resolved until after it had ended, involved H F Crowther-Smith, described by Richard Rothwell as 'a better artist than a croquet player'. Crowther-Smith had won a Cup at Woking in 1914, and he refused to return it until he had a chance to defend his title. I don't think that sounds too unreasonable, but the Woking Club applied to the Council of the Association for money to bring an action against him. However, Crowther-Smith continued to hang on to the Cup until 1918. As he'd resigned from the Association by this time anyway, the Council refused to re-admit him until he apologised, which he finally did in 1924. He also wrote a weighty tome on the game, and a couple of comic books. He edited the *Croquet Gazette* for seventeen years, only giving up the job in 1954, but his real contribution was his uncluttered, humorous line and watercolour drawings of contemporaries at play.

This fruitful period of development and re-establishment came to an abrupt end in August 1914. And just as the Great War dealt the death blow to the England of the leisured class, the country-house party, and the system which supported them, so croquet, in many ways the symbol of that era, was undermined as well.

6 CROQUET PERSONALITIES

UP TO DATE

Surprisingly, croquet probably recovered from the effects of the Great War more quickly than it did from the arrival of lawn tennis, but the long-term effects were to be more insidious. Many pre-war players did not return to the game; many clubs which had closed as a result of the war did not re-open. Above all, the private lawns were either being cut up to make tennis courts, or gradually being sold off. It was still a relatively slow process in the twenties and thirties, but life was closing in on the 'idle rich'. There was less leisure for everyone.

Croquet, however, was not without its personalities. Sir Macpherson Robertson, a self-made sweet millionaire in Australia, presented a prize in 1925 called the MacRobertson Shield (see Appendix D) for croquet's first international competition. The first international Test match was held between England and Australia, as was the second in 1927, but by the time it was played in 1930 New Zealand had joined in. Competition remained irregular and spasmodic for many years, and there was a long break between 1937 and 1950, but at least the Test matches did not fall into abeyance, and since 1974 they have been played at four-yearly intervals, with each of the participating countries playing host in turn. In 1986 England was host.

If some kind of resolution to the differences in the rules can be achieved, perhaps the United States will be able to send a team to the 1990 MacRobertson Shield Test matches, which will probably be held in New Zealand. There may, however, be another problem: croquet is a young game in the States, and their players are nowhere near the standard of the players of the three countries currently participating.

23   The MacRobertson Shield

Perhaps it should be added as a matter of pride that in croquet at least Great Britain still leads the world.

The drawback of the MacRobertson Shield, and of the amateur status of croquet, is that players have until recently had to fund themselves for it – expenses covering not only a trip halfway across the world for some of the participants, but several weeks' living expenses while away (given that one is able to be away from one's work for that long in the first place). As late as 1969 there was no commercial or government sponsorship, and money to facilitate financing of the English team was raised among Croquet Association members. Contributions must have been high, in view of the fact that at that time the CA had only about five hundred registered associates. However, by 1982, the government was paying seventy-five per cent of the air fare through the Sports Council, and Keith Wylie, who was a member of the 1982 Test team, tells me that the tour was wholly funded from one source and another, and that all the players had to find were their personal expenses (and the time taken off work).

To return to the more feudal days of the twenties, however: the

1927 Test tour was almost unable to take place, owing to lack of funds, but the problem was solved by Sir Francis Colchester-Wemyss, who loved croquet better than he could play it, but who was as generous as he was rich, because he not only baled out the touring team in 1927, but in 1935 as well. Not very surprisingly, he became President of the CA in 1946 and held on to the job until just before his death in 1953.

Arthur Law, who began his croquet career in the early 1860s and ended it in the early 1920s, bestrode the entire early history of the game. Its 'middle period' was covered by Maurice Reckitt (1888–1980), a man who, relieved of the necessity of working (he once taught for a term in a grammar school but found he didn't take to it), was able to devote his life to his interests, of which the principal one was croquet, although he was never to be such a fine player as his near contemporary, Humphrey Hicks. Hicks is acknowledged by every modern player I have talked to to be one of croquet's really great players. The exacting Keith Wylie calls him a master of strategy.

One of the most endearing things about him, I find, was his habit of knitting while awaiting his turn, and I wonder whether he adopted this hobby purposely to take his mind off the anxieties that generally possess the outplayer: life presents us with many demands for stoicism; but few require as much as an outplayer needs.

Another player who shall be mentioned among those who were active before and after the Second World War is Montague Spencer Ell. Appallingly wounded at Loos in 1915, he had lost both his arms, but that did not stop him playing croquet. John Solomon, who part-nered him and played him, remembers him most warmly:

> He was a delightful fellow and utterly incredible. One arm was just a stump he could scratch his ear with, and he'd lost the other to just above the elbow. I used to screw the mallet into its attachment for him.

Normally, Spencer Ell had a hook-like extension attached to his stump, but for croquet a special mallet with a long metal shaft could be fixed on. He could play all kinds of shots – including rolls, which must have been terribly difficult since under normal circumstances they require crouching and gripping the mallet shaft near its base. He could even remove and reattach clips from the sides of the hoops with his feet – although he couldn't do so from the crowns of the hoops. He was also an excellent player and brought his handicap down to scratch.

It would be nice to leave Spencer Ell there – cheerful, courageous

24 Humphrey Hicks, one of the game's greatest tacticians, uses side style as he prepares to run a hoop in an autumnal tournament in the fifties. (*BBC Hulton Picture Library*)

25   John Solomon and Monty Spencer Ell, during a croquet match in the mid-fifties. (*Courtesy John Solomon*)

and conquering – but there occurred in the thirties an extremely unpleasant and almost incomprehensible incident which is also a part of his story. An opponent whom he had just beaten complained to the referee of the tournament that Ell had an unfair advantage because his 'gadget' gave him a pure swing. Solomon recalls that this extraordinary behaviour so appalled Spencer Ell that he gave up the game, and could not be persuaded to return to it until after the War. On his death in 1968, however, he bequeathed more than £4,000 to the Croquet Association, and in recognition of this the Surrey Cup was renamed the Spencer Ell Cup (see Appendix D), as it remains today.

The Second World War was not kind to croquet. Again, several clubs closed, never to reopen. Hitler spoilt the 1939 President's Cup by forcing us into war two weeks before the tournament was due to be played, and in the course of his bombing attacks on London he destroyed not only Jaques' factory, as we have seen, together with every early croquet artefact in the company's possession, but also Willie Longman's definitive library of croquet books, which becomes more

26   Keith Wylie lining up a peg-out in the Northern Championship, August, 1983. (*P L Alvey*)

of a disaster when one realises just how rare books on croquet, particularly early ones, are.

Croquet emerged from the conflict bloody but unbowed, and if some clubs went to the wall, others did not even shut down for the duration.

Then three years after the war ended croquet was given a tremendous fillip by the arrival on the scene of a player who was to be the first of a new breed – players who, if croquet were not an amateur sport, would be its professionals. Keith Wylie, who would certainly be amongst them, tells me that he believes that 'the days of gracious croquet are over; croquet will become less élite, following in the footsteps of tennis'. It's certainly possible to envisage croquet becoming like tennis in one respect: a small group of professional players, and a very large spread of enthusiastic amateurs.

In 1948 John Solomon, then a sixteen-year-old Charterhouse schoolboy, beat Lydia Elphinstone-Stone for the Longworth Cup. From that auspicious beginning he moved rapidly to the top of the game (joining the 1950 MacRobertson Shield team) and stayed there until his retirement from competitive croquet thirty years later. During his reign he won forty-eight major titles, which is still an unparalleled record. Because he joined the game so young, he forms something of a bridge between an earlier generation of players and those active now. He remembers D D Steel playing:

> I was very afraid of her and also fascinated by her style, which was very upright, side-stance of course, with her right foot turned almost at right angles to her left, heels together, and the mallet swung right over her foot.

And of Lord Tollemache he says:

> While [at Southwick] I met Lord Tollemache, for the only time I think, and well remember him saying 'shake hands with me.' I did so and he said 'that's good. A firm grip, but not like a vice. You should have a grip like a surgeon, firm, but flexible.'

He thinks it's hard to say whether croquet is too esoteric for its own good.

> People take an attitude to it without ever really knowing the game. Its bad reputation has gone before it and prejudice and ignorance do the rest.

On closer acquaintance, people who bother to pursue their interest in the game invariably find it fascinating and often wish they'd taken it up earlier. The most frequent croquet converts are those who turn to it when they feel they've grown too old for tennis – but Solomon feels that the advantage of starting young is that it facilitates acquiring technique. It's true that most of the great players have taken to it in their youth, though Patrick Cotter and Bernard Neal came to it in middle age and went on to become excellent.

Solomon came to the game at the age of five, playing golf croquet (see chapter seventeen, page 162) on his parents' lawn. His somewhat unusual 'knuckles to the front' grip, called the 'Solomon grip' derives from this time, because at the age of five he was almost smaller than the mallet and the only way he could hold it was like that. Sadly no photograph of Solomon at that stage in his career is available, but there is one of the Princess of Wales, aged ten, holding her croquet mallet in precisely the same grip.

Golf croquet at least taught him the technique of hitting a ball

27   John Solomon, one of the game's all-time top players.

properly at an early stage. His father played bowls but his mother developed an interest in croquet and took it up at Roehampton Club, where Solomon first started to play the real thing himself. The attraction of it for him lay in controlling the balls, using split shots to get each ball in precisely the right position; and in setting up and maintaining a break.

> When I first tried to pick up a four-ball break – I don't know how many dozens or hundreds of times I tried it before I made my first all-round break.

Even for the most gifted of us, progress is only achieved by work! But progress can be fast: Solomon's handicap in the 1948 season went down from fifteen to ten; in 1949 he won all three events he'd entered at Hurlingham and went down to four. A fortnight later it was down to two.

Towards the end of his tournament career, Solomon became afflicted by one of the croquet-player's chief dreads: 'hoopitis'. The problem was with gentle single-ball shots, especially through hoops; all the other, more complicated strokes were still perfectly fine. But

> if I found myself six inches in front of my hoop I *knew* I was going to go straight into the wire, and of course usually did. For some reason my wrists would give some unexplainable twist which I could not control, and the result of this was that exactly the same thing happened on short roquets.... My nerve had really gone and I realized that it was impossible to play if I was jittering in front of every hoop. There was only one way to relax myself and I tried it. I got stoned, and it worked...but I knew it was ridiculous to continue along that path and abandoned such efforts.

Perhaps it's true to say that the more instinctive the player, the more likely he is to fall prey to such an inhibition. Solomon, in his personal memoir of the game, says of his own skill:

> really it's feeling as far as I'm concerned. Once you get to a certain level and know how to play the strokes it's purely a matter of confidence. ... If I was having an off day and consciously thought about playing a stroke I couldn't play it. If I thought about something else I could play it automatically.

He also regrets the more analytical approach to the game which has appeared:

> Styles change, and must change, but I have never approved of the cerebral approach to the game which has crept in in recent years.

Keith Wylie, who, if anybody, must personify the cerebral approach, is aware of that attitude, but says:

> I don't think Solomon thought about his tactics very much, though he must have done when he was a younger man because a number of innovations are credited to him ...

Solomon still plays, and even at the modest level at which I have seen him in action he is fascinating to watch. One is reminded of a veteran professional jazz player, in total command of his instrument, and yet somehow detached from it. Maybe the image is appropriate for Solomon is a gifted musician, his principal instrument being the clarinet, though he also plays the piano and the French horn.

One of post-war croquet's more colourful characters deserves a brief mention here. Bryan Lloyd Pratt is chiefly remembered for being a very sympathetic and helpful partner to less advanced players in handicap doubles (a great and welcome talent, for there are few better ways to learn and to improve than by playing with such a partner); and for his fierce rearguard action against the democratisation of croquet. He was particularly irritated by the CA's attempts to develop the game under the sponsorship of the Sports Council, but for some unfathomable reason he was given the editorship of the *Croquet Gazette*.

Actually the magazine had simply been called *Croquet* since 1954, and its image changed to a more modern one, but for the year he was in control of it, 1970, Lloyd Pratt dragged it firmly back to the turn of the century. In fact, with its *art nouveau* cover and its Gothic print, it was rather stylish, but its arch conservatism didn't suit Bryan's peers and he was ousted after four issues.

The magazine retained the title of *Gazette* until 1985, however, when a more determinedly populist lobby reintroduced the name *Croquet*, together with a design calculated to appeal to a broader cross-section of society than Bryan would ever have tolerated. He emigrated to South Africa in 1973 and was murdered there by a young acquaintance ten years later. He was fifty-two. Croquet has thrown up few more flamboyant figures since the War.

28   Lionel Wharrad, the father of short croquet, and the man chiefly responsible for the rise in croquet's fortunes in recent years. (See page 161)

29 Nigel Aspinall winning the final of the mixed doubles championship, June, 1982, Cheltenham. (*P L Alvey*)

Nigel Aspinall, who has won the President's Cup – a tournament restricted to the top eight players – far more often than anyone else ever has, first played at the age of twelve when his father brought a croquet set home. At that time he didn't know anyone else who played but he found out about the Croquet Association through his local Citizens' Advice Bureau and took it from there – actually joining his first club at Bristol, and encouraged by the warm welcome he was given. In fact his first game was a three-sided one, so he got rather an unusual first impression, and he can remember committing a whole run of faults, including 'pushing' his ball with his mallet so that instead of making a satisfying 'thwock' it sounded like coarse sandpaper run down wood!

30 Liz Taylor, Bowdon, August 1980. (*P L Alvey*)

Although nearly as many women participate in croquet at Club level as men, and although there is absolutely no discrimination against them, it is nevertheless a fact that at the top of the game very few women have emerged at all. There hasn't been a woman player in the President's Cup since the early sixties, and the last time a woman actually won it was 1937.

Perhaps women don't come into the game young enough. If they could start to become proficient at sixteen or seventeen they could enjoy several years of good play before domesticity (if they so chose) started to make other claims on their time. With the introduction of croquet at school and university level perhaps we will see some good women players coming into the game again at last, provided that the game does not become too male-dominated at those levels. Recent lady players of stature have been Jean Jarden, Susan Wiggins, Mary Collin and Veronica Carlisle. Aspinall estimates that on an open ranking system Susan Wiggins would currently be somewhere about 20th, and Mary Collin 30th, which shows how far the ladies have still to come up.

Although it is always considered that croquet is one game in which the relatively greater strength of a man carries no serious advantage, yet there is one very long shot, right across the court, where that extra strength might count. Possibly we will see a faster development of lady players in the new variation of short croquet (see chapter seventeen, page 161), which is played on a smaller lawn, and where the long shot doesn't exist; but the fact remains that croquet prospers as an equal-opportunities game, and it would be good to see women up there with the men. After all, it *has* been done in the past.

Some women are determined to compete equally with men in the full-size game. Mary Collin is one. She started playing in 1980 and already by 1982 had won the Steel Bowl for most improved lady player. She enjoys a lot of support from her croquet-playing husband, which is certainly one reason why she is able to succeed where perhaps other women would have had to opt out. For he not only gives her moral support, but also looks after their baby son, James, when necessary, and Mary was playing five weeks after James' birth in 1985. So Mary is lucky. But she says:

> Many women lose the competitive spirit, which may be one reason why they don't win more often or improve their game. Men are well known for their competitive instinct, and can you name me one man who enjoys losing – and losing to a woman?

Though she admits that all of the men she has beaten have been gracious losers.

As for the question of relative strength, she says:

> there is no reason why women can't be as good as men; the game requires only thought, knowledge and a certain amount of skill to play ... I am not particularly strong, but am quite tall which may help ...

Above all, she stresses again, the most important prerequisite is the determination to win. Her own goal now is to become good enough to qualify for the MacRobertson Shield team.

Veronica Carlisle also feels that the competitive spirit is of prime importance. She came to the game through her husband and learnt it by watching him play at Hurlingham during the summer of 1967 when she was carrying their second child. She liked the fact that it was a still-ball game, was attracted to its intellectual demands, and liked the people who played it. She freely admits that she has been able to reach the top of the game because she has never been a working wife (in the sense of having to go out to work), and because she has always enjoyed the help of *au-pairs* at home. Thus she has had more leisure than many women to develop her game.

She remembers wrily a match during the Women's Championship not so long ago. The ladies are often rather mocked for being slower to finish a game than the men. On this particular occasion, Mrs Carlisle finished two games before lunch, which is nothing for the men, but fairly unusual for the women. She reported her results to the tournament manager. He, only giving her half his attention, said, 'Well done – go and have lunch and then get on again', because he assumed that she couldn't possibly have finished before lunch. She had, in fact, won two games in a best of three match and it gave her great pleasure to put him right.

One of Mrs Carlisle's other pleasant memories is that of partnering Kitty Godfree, in whom the determination to win is still alive at the age of ninety.

7 SOCIAL CROQUET

The last chapter emphasised the competitive aspects of contemporary croquet, but it would be a pity if because of the game's increasing appeal as a competitive sport its origins in social fun were altogether forgotten.

In its first flush of youth, croquet was essentially a sociable game, as this description – from a contemporary rule-book of a croquet party in 1870 indicates:

A large and merry party were assembled, on one of the most beautiful of Autumnal afternoons, on the spacious lawn in the centre of the grounds surrounding the residence of Captain Moreton, of Eastwood-house.

The occasion of this happy gathering, was, we believe, owing to the fact that on this day the anniversary of Miss Moreton's birth-day was to be honoured, that young lady having reached her fourteenth year.

A right good party had met to do honour to the young lady, and join in wishing her 'many happy returns of the day'.

The ladies were all, of course, very elegantly attired, some in the most modern and loveable of Croquêt costume – the bloomer. All, however, who were determined upon a good game of Croquêt came suitably attired for the party on the lawn, and exhibited their pretty ancles (sic) and neatly made tight-fitting red

31 A croquet tournament at Highgate in 1869, chiefly remarkable for the high number of
spectators. (*Mary Evans Picture Library*)

boots, with strong soles; and those ladies not habited in full
Croquêt costume, had taken the necessary precaution to so loop
up their dresses, that they might form no impediment to the
progress of the game. The young gentlemen were not, of course,
behind hand on this occasion, for they were all, without exception,
dressed in the height of Croquêt fashion, viz. in the prettiest dress
that has ever been invented, *i.e.* in light knickerbocker suits, caps
to match, cricketers' shoes without spikes, &c &c. We do not
remember ever having seen a more interesting and charming
group of merry young folks.

If this account inspires you to organise your own croquet party,
the *Girls' Own Paper* of June 1880 can provide a suggestion for a suitable
lunch:

Butter should be moulded into balls, and parsley taken to garnish
it after being set out. A cold shoulder of lamb is an excellent joint
... accompanied by a bottle of mint sauce.

32   Croquet at the Duke of Richmond's castle in the 1860s. Note the size of both mallets and hoops. (*BBC Hulton Picture Library*)

It is perhaps better to have the ham ready sliced.

Meat pies, and pigeon, and veal and ham pies are standard. ... In all pies, the gravy within should be strong enough to form a jelly when cold.

Lobster, the meat picked out and carried in the main shell, with mayonnaise and salad separately (it is thought expensive, perhaps?) but fish dishes, such as eel moulded in jelly, are cool.

Cold roast ducks are sure to be popular, and cold dressed green peas not to be despised with them. We have known people take cold new potatoes, but did not consider them a success.

A well-made salad everyone will enjoy, and a cucumber is indispensable!

Jellies and creams and compot of fruit, with a mould of well boiled rice, are excellent. ... Claret cup is sure to be wanted, to be mixed on the spot by one of the gentlemen.

If you decide that you would like to serve Claret cup, here is a recipe: one large teaspoonful of white sugar dissolved in boiling water, one glass of sherry, half a glass of brandy, half a glass of maraschino, a thin rind of lemon and a strip of cucumber rind all to each bottle of claret. Let the mixture (stirred together gently) stand for an hour in a cool place. Set the bowl on crushed ice and add a sprig of borage, which has a splendid aroma. Remove the sprig when serving, and top up with seltzer or plain Perrier water, as you please. (I'd suggest letting the guests do their own topping up to taste.)

However, if your catering skills don't extend beyond bread and cheese and beer, don't be deterred. Croquet isn't sacrosanct. Also, there are more essential aspects to be considered. For example, correct pairing at doubles is a very important question and one whose psychological effect can lead to triumph or disaster whether croquet is being played at tournament, business, or purely 'fun' level.

If you should happen to be organising a croquet party, and find yourself in the position of having to pair people up for a game of doubles who do not know each other well, use the notes which follow as a guide, together with your own knowledge of the temperaments involved. Then sort everyone out roughly along the lines of whom you might seat next to whom at a dinner party.

There are two kinds of doubles play: the sort in which you are of the same standard as your partner, and the sort in which your standard is much higher or lower than your partner's.

In the second case, much will depend on your own temperament and on finding its correct counterpart. The 'senior' partner must be patient and confident, and above all relaxed. He should have the qualities of a good teacher or instructor, but he should never let his 'junior' partner feel that he himself has nothing to contribute. An ideal senior partner is a rare find – since he must also be philosophical when his junior cocks things up. In addition to all these saintly qualities he must be able to plan the whole game's strategy, and to play to set favourable 'leaves' and pick-upable breaks for his weaker half. The junior partner, too, must ideally be super-human: he must combine concentration and a desire to do his best with humility, patience, and a willingness to learn. Given these near-impossible *desiderata*, handicap doubles can be enormously rewarding for both parties.

Level doubles is more straightforward to explain, but just as difficult to achieve: briefly, your partner should be absolutely on your wavelength. By that I mean someone who really feels the game as you do. The ideal partner in this context is one with whom you barely need to consult, so identically do you both think, but given that this *is* an ideal rather a reality, discussion can be kept to a minimum by an intelligent assessment of the lie of the balls. They should tell you all that you need to know to make your next turn effective for your side. Most players tend to have a steady partner, and a relationship that has grown up over many games played together. I think that the root of the best partnership lies in friendship; there are family teams – husband and wife, mother and son, for example – but perhaps these pairings are too vulnerable to volatile emotion to be predictably successful.

Two final points about handicap doubles: if you are the senior partner, it is up to you to decide whether to (a) get your junior round first, (b) get round first yourself, (c) take him round with you. Factors will be the temperament of your partner and the relative unity of your opposing team (also, of course, composed of a senior and a junior). The second point is that in handicap doubles the senior may not peel the junior through more than four hoops.

You may, of course, decide to go for golf croquet. The advantage of this is that it is a game that can be picked up quickly by someone who hasn't ever held a mallet before. Mrs Frances Yorke Batley of Boscombe has been giving golf croquet parties for members of the acting profession since 1949, during which time 11,000 thespians have taken tea and wielded a mallet on her lawn. The D'Oyly Carte Opera Company were regular visitors for twenty-four years, and other artists who've played croquet with Mrs Yorke Batley while appearing at the Bournemouth Pavilion include Sean Connery (*South Pacific*, 1954), Vera Lynn and Spike Milligan.

There is a collection of about thirty albums of photographs – all but the most recent taken in black and white with Mrs Yorke Batley's box-Brownie – recording not only the last forty years of actors, but of changing fashion too. Only the croquet sets remain unchanged – though Mrs Yorke Batley's companion, Miss Meade, shows gentle distress at the recollection of how some of the actors mishandled the mallets! The collection of photographs is a private one, but is to be left to the Theatre Museum, together with the dozen or so visitors' books that accompany it.

The croquet parties came about when Mrs Yorke Batley's husband, then Rector at Corfe Castle, was persuaded by his bishop to become Actors' Church Union chaplain for the area. Tea and croquet became a regular thing every Friday for actors touring or doing weekly rep in Bournemouth right up until the Reverend Yorke Batley's death

in 1960. At that point, Mrs Yorke Batley felt she should give it up, but
Leslie Crowther dissuaded her, and so she has continued, though the
tea parties have now become coffee mornings.

At the start of every summer, Miss Meade repaints the hoops,
and brings out the two venerable Jaques boxwood croquet sets, one
purchased at the beginning of Mrs Yorke Batley's own croquet career,
the other inherited from her step-father, from whom she learnt the
game. Various admirers and friends down the years have given the two
ladies additional mallets: the square-headed brass-bound ones look quite
flashy. Mrs Yorke Batley has her lawn weeded and re-seeded annually.
She remembers the lawn figuring in one of Hinge and Bracket's sketches
in a television show – Evadne, buried in the local paper, reads out:
'Mrs Yorke Batley has moles on her croquet lawn.' 'I've been chipped
about that often since,' she says.

She is a life-long croquet player herself, and since for most of his
ministry her husband was appointed to vicarages with large gardens
she has been able to create a lawn wherever she's been 'except for fifteen
dreadful years in Kent'. She remembers more than one occasion on
which the weekly croquet party has provided the necessary impetus for
a hitherto unhappy touring company to relax and for its members to
make friends with each other.

Until recently, the parties were fuelled on nothing more than tea
and cakes – Miss Meade's cakes are so delicious that Spike Milligan,
after his fourth slice, once decided to propose. They used to supply
boiled eggs too – up to forty at a time, for the parties were not small.

> I used to boil to order and had several saucepans – one for three
> minuters, one for three-and-a-half-minuters, and one for four-
> minuters. But it really was rather a bind and so in the end we
> scrapped that and just did four-minute eggs in two enormous chip
> pans. No-one complained.

Recently, the format of the parties has changed. The actors arrive
for coffee, then play croquet until midday when they stop for sherry.
Mrs Yorke Batley remembers that once or twice one of the attendant
chaplains has been a little too pressing with the sherry,

> ... and occasionally one or two girls have had a drop too much –
> and so I told him, we can't have that, because I can't have them
> coming up here and then going off, you know, a bit squiffy. It

wouldn't do. He's been very careful since. He was just over-anxious to make the party go and he rather overdid it.

She finds theatrical people neither noticeably good nor noticeably bad at the game, though many left determined to play more after their introduction to it. In forty years, she cannot recall any displays of ill-temper on the lawn. Vintage years were 1976, when all the Tiller girls came and played, and 1984, when at the suggestion of Rolf Harris she abandoned her box brownie for a new camera, and burst into colour film. She is still rather doubtful about this move, though, 'not being a person for change'. Among her favourite guests are Peter Barkworth, Millicent Martin, and Wilfred Hyde White.

If you are playing just for fun, it doesn't matter too much if your lawn slopes a bit or has the odd bump in it. At Peterhouse, Cambridge, the lawns certainly used to slope quite dramatically, and at Magdalene a large tree grew in the middle of the court and had to be used as the peg. At Clare, an Anthony Caro sculpture entitled 'Sunrise' was placed in the middle of the lawn used for croquet outside Memorial Court and had to be accommodated into the game, becoming a rather large hoop to be run, though it was tough on the player whose ball stuck underneath – he was allowed a 'cue-stroke' *in extremis*.

On the whole, however, avoid large, permanent obstacles, like rockeries. Trees can be a bore, too; but rather than not playing croquet, or (worse) cutting the trees down, invent your own local rule to cover ricochet. Croquet is a most adaptable, amenable game, and though you will get most out of it if you play the real rules, don't let them get in the way of having fun when you're playing informally. Alternatively, at a party, use one of the variations mentioned in chapter seventeen – or invent your own, the simplicity of the equipment offers a plethora of choice.

Finally, I hope that when you do throw your croquet party you won't find that Mr Justice Bargrave Deane was indeed correct. He had been hearing a case for judicial separation brought by a Mrs Alice Mary Fearnley-Whittingstall against her husband. The *International Herald Tribune* of 29 October 1909 reported as follows:

> It was alleged that the rector frequently lost his temper, and his wife had stated that on one occasion when they were playing croquet he was so annoyed because she raised a question as to whether his ball had quite gone through a hoop that he did not speak to her for days.

Commented the judge, whether in exasperation or in sympathy is not certain: 'I do not think there is any game which is so liable to put one out of humour as croquet.'

8 CROQUET OBSERVED

For such a noble game, it is odd that croquet has been noticed so little in literature, although this neglect has been made up for in one way: most games attract a certain amount of bad eulogistic poetry from their admirers, but none has collected as much as croquet! The pages of the *Gazette* are littered with contributions, all kindly meant, but most better forgotten – and certainly unquotable, for, truly arcane, they contain innumerable references to people and events totally unknown outside the croquet world. The worst offender in terms of quantity, if not quality, in recent times was Maurice Reckitt himself – one of the truly grand old men of the game. The odd thing is that a lot of the amateur poets of croquet use the most sophisticated and difficult poetic forms.

In the Victorian era, Trollope refers to croquet in *The Small House At Allington*; and in *Lothair* Disraeli sends his young hero to a match: his hero, Lothair, is a vastly wealthy orphan nobleman Oxbrite; in the descriptions of croquet Disraeli picks out one or two nice social details:

> It was a great croquet family, the Brentham family; even listless Lord St. Aldegonde would sometimes play, with a cigar never out of his mouth. They did not object to his smoking in the air ...
>
> There was a great croquet party one morning at Brentham. Some neighbours had been invited who loved the sport. Mr. Blenkinsop, a grave young gentleman, whose countenance never relaxed while he played, and who was understood to give his mind entirely up to croquet ... was the owner of the largest estate

in the country, and it was thought he would very willingly have allied himself with one of the young ladies of the house of Brentham; but these flowers were always so quickly plucked that his relations with the distinguished circle never grew more intimate than croquet. He drove over with some fine horses and several cases and bags containing instruments for the fray. His sister came with him, whom it was thought he would not allow to marry because he would miss her so much in his favourite pastime . . .

It seemed to Lothair a game of great deliberation and of more interest than gaiety, though sometimes a cordial cheer, and sometimes a ringing laugh of amiable derision notified a signal triumph or a disastrous failure. But the scene was brilliant; a marvellous lawn, the Duchess' Turkish tent with its rich hangings, and the players themselves, the prettiest of all the spectacle, with their coquettish hats and their half-veiled and half-revealed under-raiment, scarlet and silver, or blue and gold, made up a sparkling and modish scene.

Lothair was published in 1870, by which time croquet had indeed become 'a game of great deliberation and of more interest than gaiety'. It is tempting, given the tenuous connection, to put Walter Jones Whitmore into the role of technical adviser to Disraeli for this description – or even to see a caricature of him in Mr Blenkinsop. But it is not very likely that either is truly the case.

As Walter himself seems not to have used poetry or prose to hymn his game, the only other Victorian who referred to game at all seriously in fictional work was Carroll. *Alice's Adventures Under Ground* was the first version of *Alice's Adventures in Wonderland*, and for it he drew the illustrations himself. It's a pity that he felt them not good enough for publication, because they are a lot livelier than Tenniel's, but the famous croquet match is unchanged in the later version – except for one detail. In *Alice's Adventures Under Ground* the game is played with hedgehogs and *ostriches*. The actual description is far too well known to need repeating. Both *Under Ground* and *Wonderland* were completed before 1866 – the year of the *Field* croquet laws and the year from which croquet assumed its more serious form. That is possibly why Alice's croquet game is still a scene of such uproarious anarchy.

Further afield, Tolstoy used a croquet match at the house of a morally lax countess as the backdrop for a meeting between Anna

33   The game of Croquet: one of the original drawings by Lewis Carroll for *Alice's Adventures Under Ground* – the book which subsequently became *Alice's Adventures in Wonderland*. (*Courtesy of the British Library*)

Karenina and Vronsky. He was writing the book in the early 1870s, when the game was at the height of its popularity. Garbo played possibly the sultriest croquet game on record with Frederic March in the 1935 film of the novel.

Moving on slightly, Chesterton wrote an elegant short story called *The Perfect Game*, and H G Wells gave us a rather dreary novella, *The Croquet Player*, in 1936, in which croquet really might as well have been any other game. Written under the approaching shadow of Nazism, Wells made the relative triviality of an appointment to play croquet with his aunt the only secure refuge in the life of a weak young man too long protected from the real world. The plot unfolds in an atmosphere of dismal pessimism, full of such lines as 'Man is still what he was, invincibly bestial, envious, malicious, greedy'; and somewhere a psychiatrist has the rather splendid line: 'What does croquet matter if your world is falling in ruins about you?' *Bona si sua norint*.

The most recent, and indeed the only other substantial use of croquet in literature (there are others too minor to mention) lies in a comedy thriller, *A Rush On the Ultimate*, by H R F Keating, published in 1961. This is an extremely quirky piece of work from the man who went on to write the Inspector Ghote novels. It centres on a croquet party which is spread over a week and forms an annual feature in the summer lives of half a dozen amiable eccentrics – one of whom is found one morning battered to death with a croquet mallet.

One is not surprised to learn that Maurice Reckitt was Keating's technical advisor, for the book is full of croquet lore and jargon, as the following extract shows:

> 'But there's one thing you really ought to know', said Humphrey. 'And that's the story of what the timid man heard outside the croquet club.'
>
> He flourished his mallet in anticipation.
>
> 'All right, I'll take it,' said Ned.
>
> 'Well, there was this chap, as I say, rather timid, and he happened to overhear what the first old dear said to the second old dear. And this was it. Now listen carefully. "It was just a question of which of us would peg out first; I hit her again and again; she was black and blue and when she thought she'd got me tied up in a corner I saw red, got my shot in, and rushed towards her, first with a cut and then a split, and soon it was all over."'
>
> 'Good on you,' Ned said.

Although Victorian cartoonists had a field day with croquet, artists of the period barely touched it. Dégas preferred the race-track and Lautrec and Seurat the circus. Edouard Manet, however, took croquet as his subject on two occasions in the 1870s, showing very accurately the awful condition of the lawns, and nearly twenty years later his sister-in-law, Berthe Morisot, painted *Croquet à Mezy*.

J J J Tissot painted the subject in the late 1870s – though the principal girl in his picture looks out at you with an expression that suggests doing something that's a lot more fun than hitting a ball with a mallet. The details are good. Note the small head on the mallet, and the striped balls. At about the same time, Kaemmerer painted a *Croquet Party*, and Thomas Hill produced *Palo Alto Spring*.

The chief croquet artist, however, was the American, Winslow Homer, who completed a large number of engravings and five oils, some of quite substantial size, in the 1860s, presumably before croquet fell into disrepute in America. The sexuality of Tissot's girl (one shouldn't forget the main reason for croquet's popularity in the nineteenth century) is far less apparent in Homer's graceful, static figures, and his croquet scenes convey all the gentle calm of a Corot landscape. This is intensified by the long shadows and deep light, suggesting that the games were played in the temperate late afternoons.

34 Edouard Manet, *Partie de Croquet*, 1873. (*Courtesy of the Staedlsches Kunstinstitut, Frankfurt am Main*)

35 Winslow Homer, *A Game of Croquet*, 1866. One of his series on the game. (*Courtesy of Yale University Art Gallery. Bequest of Stephen Carlton Clark, BA, 1903.*)

36   James Jaques Joseph Tissot: *Croquet*, oil on canvas, *c*. 1878. The most delicately erotic treatment of the game as a backdrop to courtship. (*Courtesy of The Art Gallery of Hamilton, Ontario. Gift of Dr and Mrs Basil Bowman in memory of their daughter, Suzanne, 1965.*)

37   Watercolour by John Nash, *A Game of Croquet*, 1913. (*Courtesy of Spink and Son*)

In the twentieth century John Nash painted the game in 1913, and John Sloan painted an oil, 'Croquet', in 1918. Christopher Sproat created a large free-form sculpture, 'Contemplating Croquet' in 1981. Popular art, advertising and cartoons, have all touched on the game, much more obviously in the USA than in Great Britain, and possibly because of the perennial popularity there of the 'backyard' game.

Because the game was so popular, it did not escape the attention either of the music hall. On the whole the songs stressed the *real* reason for playing croquet – that is, dalliance. Here are the words and music of some of them, without any further comment from me.

CROQUET
by John B Lawreen
Composed by Vincent Davis
Sung by J H Milburn

Voice. Tempo: Schotische

A friend of mine asked me, one day if I'd go, To his snug lit-tle box out of town. The in - vite I ac-cep-ted and star-ted next day By the nine for-ty five ex-press down. I soon reach'd his place, and he then said to me, My dear boy while with us you stay You can boat, shoot or fish, do just what you wish, On con-di-tion that at cro-quet you play.

Chorus

At cro-quet, cro-quet, A pro-per game to play! At cro-quet, cro-quet, I could play all day, There's no-thing can sur-pass, The sport up-on the grass. In that aw-ful jol-ly game call'd cro-quet.

Published by Duff & Stewart

A nice little party he had at his house
And each sunny day as a treat
At Croquet we'd play with such dear little Girls
Who in short dresses shew'd pretty feet,
Soon one I selected as partner for play

Such a duck as a partner for life
I croqueted the balls and croqueted the hoops
And I tried to croquet her for my wife.

       At croquet . . .

Young De Bounce of the Blues didn't like it at all
For with my partner he played as a rule
So like knights of old we retir'd to a wood
And with our mallets then fought a duel.
We fenced and we fought till he cried 'Hold enough –
The lady I'll resign unto you.
Tho' many years in the Blues I have been
I'm now beaten black as well as blue.'

       At croquet . . .

Then back to my partner, a victor I went
And at croquet and love play'd my part.
When we'd beat all the rest I thought it the best
To at once make a stroke for her heart.
We'd gone thro' the hoops, and struck both the post
When I ask'd her to be mine for life
So well I'd play'd my part, I'd croqueted her heart
And a Gold hoop soon made her my Wife.

       At croquet . . .

'CROQUET': *Ladies' Version* by Thos. W Charles
In many jolly games, we Girls love to join,
The best I declare of them all
Is darling croquet, that glorious sport,
That is played with the mallet and ball.
'Tis then, you must know, that we flirt and coquet,
With our partners so handsome and gay,
No doubt it is the game, the men's hearts to tame,
If at croquet we can get them to play,

   At croquet, at croquet, we pass time away,
   In garden or on green, there never yet has been
   Such an awful jolly game as croquet.

Whenever I'm at play, all eyes then are turn'd,
On this neat little figure and face,
As I pose with the grace of a fairy to drive,
Some enemy far from the base.

With a fast or a slow, through the hoops then I go,
Such skill all declare they've ne'er seen,
In fact, 'mongst our set of men, I'm the pet,
And they say that at croquet I am Queen.
  Then it's croquet . . .

Now you'd hardly think that I'd by Cupid been caught,
But alas 'tis a fact I must own,
An awful swell fellow, a friend of Papa's,
Thought at croquet he'd play me alone,
I need scarcely say, that he stood not a chance,
But love made me play a sad part,
For I let him beat me, so pleas'd then was he
That I croqueted my way to his heart.
  Then it's croquet . . .

And now before I go, a word I must say,
To all my dear sisters so fair,
If a chance you should get, then like me make a *hit*,
For the plain golden hoop that we wear,
To shew to the world, that we've battled and won,
By the aid of our darling croquet
A husband so dear, that there's then little fear,
Of a lifetime so happy and gay.
  Then it's croquet . . .

CROQUET
by C H Webb
Composed by J R Thomas

Out on the lawn in the eve-ning gray Went Wil-lie and Kate, I

said 'which way?' And they both re-plied, 'Cro - quet', 'cro-quet'.

Of mal-let and balls the us-ual dis-play, The

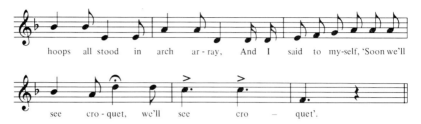

hoops   all stood   in   arch   ar-ray,   And   I   said   to   my-self, 'Soon we'll
see   cro-quet,   we'll   see   cro   —   quet'.

Published by Wm A Pond & Co.

But the mallet and balls unheeded lay,
And the maid and the youth side by side sat they,
And I thought to myself –
Is that croquet?
I saw the scamp, it was bright as day,
Put his arm around her waist in a loving way,
And he squeezed her hand, –
Was that croquet? Was that croquet?

While the red rover roll'd all forgotten away,
He whisper'd all that a lover should say,
And kiss'd her lips –
What a queer croquet!
Silent they sat 'neath the moon of May,
But I knew by her blushes she said not nay,
And I thought in my heart,
Now that's croquet! Now that's croquet.

And as we are back with the Victorians, I will close this chapter with
a verse from a poem by Clement Scott. On the subject of the unknown
origins of the game, the poet supposes that the gods of Olympus
compete to invent the best game of all. It concludes:

Little Cupid, for a minute, had escaped from Aphrodite,
    Very plump and very hearty, as all honest love should be,
And he said, 'I've found a game out, never slow and never flighty,
    And it's capable of skill as well as spooning, as you'll see.'
Then he sang a song of croquet, of its present and hereafter,
    With such exquisite persuasion, and such mischief in his eyes,
That the deities, delighted, shook Olympus with their laughter,
    And to Cupid was awarded, for his impudence, the prize!

PART TWO

9 JOHN JAQUES & SON

Although there are now several manufacturers of croquet equipment, the name of Jaques is synonymous with the game and a history of the company and a description of equipment manufacture are appropriate in this book.

Jaques is the oldest manufacturer of sports equipment in the world. Not only has the company survived and prospered since its foundation in 1795, but it has remained a solidly family firm – the business having been handed down six generations (so far) from father to son – an extraordinary record. Not exclusively manufacturers of croquet equipment, the company is responsible for many parlour games which one might have thought had had no single originator, so much have they become part of the British way of life. 'Happy Families', 'Snakes & Ladders', 'Ping Pong', 'Ludo', and 'Tiddley Winks' are among their inventions and developments, and today they manufacture equipment for archery, bowls, snooker, shove ha'penny, hockey, table tennis, and much more. As if this were not enough, the firm is also responsible for the original 'Staunton' chessmen. But it is for their connection with croquet that Jaques are best known.

The company was started by the twenty-one-year-old Thomas Jaques, a young man of Huguenot descent who had come down to London from the village of Grittleton, near Chippenham, to seek his fortune. He'd got himself apprenticed to a bone and ivory turner called Ivy, who worked at 65 Leather Lane, in 1789. Five years later Mr Ivy died, and Thomas, having learnt the trade, promptly married Ivy's niece and started business on his own account as a 'Manufacturer of

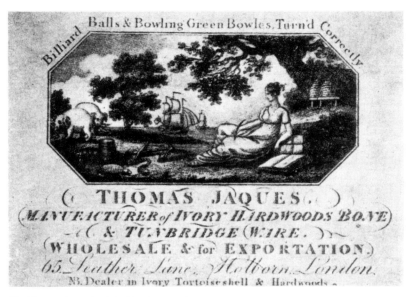

38   Thomas Jaques' original business card. (*Courtesy Jaques and Son*)

Ivory, Hardwoods, Bone and Tunbridge Ware'. His business card reflects the breadth of his ambitions – ships represent the potential 'exportation' side of the business; two doughty elephants remind you of the ivory in which he principally worked; a Greek goddess seems to be about to sign a contract; and a couple of beehives symbolise industry. Thomas quickly expanded the scope of the company, producing goods ranging from carved snuff-boxes to hairbrushes, from paperknives to glove-stretchers.

A son was born in 1795. This was John Jaques I, who joined the firm as a partner in 1816. The company became 'T & J Jaques, Wholesale Ivory Turners', but they were already dealing in hardwoods, and the business was to become timber-based, as it remains today. Lignum vitae appears for the first time, as does the Turkey box wood which some time later would be used in the manufacture of croquet mallets and balls. A greatly expanded list of products includes some intriguing items: 'Pope Joan tables', and (by 1838) 'Sea-horse teeth' for dentists. Sea-horse teeth were so called because they were false teeth made from hippopotamus ivory.

John Jaques I (or JJ-One, as he's familiarly known) married, and produced John Jaques II, who joined the firm himself and who, as we know, was largely responsible for the dissemination of croquet in

England. But his father has an equally great claim to fame for his contribution to chess. In 1839, shortly after the company had expanded its premises to Hatton Garden, he designed a new set of chessmen, having identified a gap in the market. Hitherto players had either had to buy extremely ornate and expensive sets, or cheap, but very crude ones. Jaques' designs, prepared in collaboration with his father-in-law, Nathaniel Cooke, proprietor of *The Illustrated London News*, differentiated the pieces well, but remained simple enough to be mass-produced at a relatively low price. The king is represented by a crown, the queen by a coronet, and the bishops by a mitre. The knights' heads were copied from the recently-arrived Elgin Marbles, and the pawn was designed to represent the masonic emblem of a square and compasses. The set takes its name from Howard Staunton, the contemporary grandmaster, who was so impressed that he agreed to associate himself with the design, and it remains the standard international design for chessmen, though many other firms worldwide have since borrowed it for manufacture.

John Jaques II was not only responsible for croquet. He also introduced 'Happy Families', and commissioned John Tenniel, who later drew the illustrations for the 'Alice' books, to draw the characters for the cards. There is another, later, Lewis Carroll connection with the company too. The present managing director's grandfather, John Jaques III, was widowed. He remarried Irene Dodgson, Carroll's grand-niece.

John Jaques III joined the firm in 1884. He was a great athlete, and expanded the production of tennis, cricket, football, hockey, badminton and archery equipment. He also picked up a new game called 'Gossima', re-marketed it under the name 'Ping-Pong', and watched it enjoy a boom in Edwardian England. As the game began to be taken more seriously, however, its name was changed to 'Table Tennis', which was thought more dignified. Under 'JJ-Three', the company increasingly became what it is today, as the emphasis of its output shifted towards sporting equipment and away from parlour games, which were beginning to decline in popularity by the twenties and thirties. John Jaques III died in 1937 and was succeeded by his son, John Jaques IV. In the same year Fred 'Spider' Webster joined the company. He is still with Jaques, and is now their master turner.

The war, when it came, brought a mixture of disaster and salvation for the company. Jaques and many of their competitors experienced a slump in 1939. Not only did the market for sports equipment collapse,

39   John Jaques I. (*Courtesy Jaques and Son*)

40   John Jaques II, the man chiefly responsible for the popularisation of croquet in Great Britain. (*Courtesy Jaques and Son*)

41   John Jaques V (left) and Christopher Jaques, who currently manage the company and represent the sixth generation to do so. (*Courtesy Jacques and Son*)

but the materials needed to make the equipment ceased to be readily available. Help, however, was at hand from an unusual and unexpected source. The War Department approached the company with a contract for secret work. The work involved making games – mainly board games – in which files, hacksaw blades, compasses and maps were concealed. The games were packed into Red Cross parcels for despatch to prisoners-of-war. The escape aids were so well concealed that it must have been almost impossible to find them; but servicemen would be forewarned at home of their existence, and told how to locate them in the event of their being taken prisoner.

The secret work provided a lifeline for the company, because the War Office naturally granted special licences for it to obtain materials not otherwise available for such 'non-essential' equipment as games, and clearly no German spy was perceptive enough to put two and two together. However, in 1941 Jaques' Hatton Garden factory, which they'd occupied for just over a hundred years, was badly ·bombed. All the equipment and all the company records, save for one ancient pattern-book, were destroyed. Today, Christopher Jaques keeps an eye out for nineteenth century croquet equipment made by the company: none left in stock survived the air-raid, and little appears to have survived in general. Any owner of an ivory mallet would be strongly advised to contact him!

Christopher Jaques remembers his father's own reminiscence about turning the familiar corner of the familiar street to see a gaping hole where his factory had been; but JJ-Four immediately started the search for new premises. He found two possible sites, and plumped for a derelict shoe-factory in Croydon, Surrey. Once again, the War Office acted as *deus ex machina* and provided a local builder with all the materials he needed to convert and renovate the factory, and within a month of the Hatton Garden disaster, Jaques were operational in their new home, which remains their base to this day, though the company has expanded to a second factory. Jaques continued to fulfil its secret contract throughout the war, but they weren't exclusively making games for Red Cross parcels – that would have attracted the attention of the dullest German spy – but manufacturing regular sports equipment as well, and enjoying the benefits of a relatively competition-free market. The company celebrated its 150th anniversary in 1945 in a buoyant mood.

Since the war Jaques has continued to expand quietly, and recently took over Webber Footballs and also introduced *boules* to their product-list. Croquet nonetheless remains an important part of their output, and they retain their position as 'the original and still the best' manufacturers, quietly supporting a world market from the Croydon factory. The factory itself is a surprise – tucked away behind a busy road, it looks tiny from the outside, and almost abandoned. Inside, you discover a labyrinthine succession of rooms and workshops, in which all manner of sports equipment is made. Everywhere there is the whine of lathes and the smell of wood.

When I first visited the factory a consignment of lignum vitae had just come in. Each of the logs, which were relatively small – you can't get mature lignum any more – weighed about 3 cwt, and each took three men to lift, though they only measured about 3 feet 10 inches long and 9 inches in diameter. Such a log will yield four square mallet heads per 9 inches of its length. Immediately after delivery, the logs are cut into blanks – rectangles of wood $\frac{1}{4}$ inch over the finished size, to allow for shrinkage – and then stored for two to two and a half years to dry. The drying process cannot be hurried since lignum is so dense it would crack. No round-headed lignum mallets are produced any more because the wood is now too costly for the wastage involved in producing a round head. Round-headed 'blanks' are also rectangular – though naturally rather larger.

It is sad to think that lignum may soon become unavailable, because it's a beautiful wood. Grayish-green in life, the finished mallet-head it produces is burnished to a dark brown-gold with a distinctive grain. It has been overfelled and, because it is a very slow-growing tree which does not grow straight, it has not been replaced – though Christopher Jaques suspects that there may still be substantial pockets left, protected by the governments of the countries where it grows more to keep its price up than to conserve it. Jaques have another problem with lignum. In order to provide local labour, the South and Central American governments involved do not want to export raw logs but to sell only turned cylinders of timber: this also enables them to add a local labour content to its price. The problem with this is that the timber millers there don't know how to select the right part of the log to cut, and in any case don't know how to cut it.

Most hardwoods, including lignum, have what is called a 'heart shake' – a cross-shaped crack running through the heart of the wood. Mallet heads have to be cut *around* the centre of the tree to avoid this. Proper cutting is quite an art, and you need to have a raw log to work from, where the shake is naturally located in its centre. A turned

42   Lignum vitae – logs in Jaques'
yard waiting to be turned into
croquet mallet heads. (*Courtesy Jaques
and Son*)

cylinder of wood will ignore the natural form of the tree, and is thus
useless for Jaques' purposes. What is more, cutting the mallet heads
must be done to minimise wastage of wood. The biggest lignum trunks
available today are barely twelve inches across. Also, lignum not only
grows twistily, but the width of its trunk varies along its length. It may
be the prince of hardwoods but it doesn't grow to accommodate Man.
In view of the fact that lignum may not be around much longer, or
may become prohibitively expensive, Jaques retain two dendrologists
to research other hardwoods. At present one or two – whose names
must remain secret – are being considered and tested.

     After two and a half years one of a batch of blanks is tested with
a moisture-meter to check the relative dryness of the batch. Drying is
calculated at about one inch a year. If they are dry enough they are cut
to their correct size, and a boxwood sightline inlaid along their tops.
The turners then carve the concentric circular grooving on the faces of
the mallet head (which permit greater 'grip' on the ball – also grooved –
during impact-contact). The heads are then left for a further three

months for the sightline to settle. They are then fine-polished, and any sightline-outcrop is trimmed off. The turners will also fit brass binding rings at this stage on those mallet heads which have them. A hole is bored in the head and the shaft split, fitted, wedged, and glued before a final polish and varnish. Much of the turning and assembling process is machine-assisted, but the inlaying of the sightline, cane-splicing the shaft, stringing the handle, and final assembly are all done by hand.

The shafts are turned on a lathe, even the octagonal handle being cut by a special programmable lathe fitted with the most lethal set of blades I've ever seen and making a noise like all the devils in hell.

A mallet can be 'compiled' to a special weight specification to within an ounce. A skilled assembler will know the weight of each separate component right down to the handle-string on a top-market mallet, and be able to assemble a mallet to overall correct weight by balancing the weights of the individual components. The heaviest single element is the head. The other heavy element (as you might expect) is the cost of such special service: but if you want a Rolls Royce, you don't expect to pay for a Mini. Most people, however, will be happy to buy a middle-of-the-range mallet with a round head entirely made of English ash. This will not come with a brass-bound head with milled faces but – in the right hands – it will still get a ball through a hoop.

The bulk of Jaques' croquet business lies in selling complete croquet sets for ordinary family use. Perhaps surprisingly, though, sets sell right across the cost range; apparently because there are people who can afford a 'Hurlingham' or an 'Association' set and go for it simply because it is the best. General advice on equipment is given in Appendix A, but I'd advise anyone who was aiming to play the game within the family and for fun to go for a middle-range set, which will last a lifetime given the proper (minimal) care. And if you get bitten by the croquet bug, then you can go to Jaques and buy yourself an individual mallet for £100 plus! Even that's not bad, compared to some tennis racquets I have seen.

Hoops and balls are supplied in various categories, which I will deal with in general in Appendix A. Before leaving Jaques, though, I must mention one of the mallets from their 1910 catalogue: it was 'the Venetian' – 'a very smart and attractive pattern, with black head and handle, bound in red cord'. The deluxe version was fitted with plated metal rings at the ends and cost 12/6d. The manufacturers advise: 'These mallets should be carried in cases to prevent their being soiled. Price 4/6d extra.' Clearly, far too pretty to use!

VENETIAN MALLET.

A very smart and attractive pattern.

Black Head and Handle, bound red cord.

		£	s.	d.

No. 1. Stained Boxwood Head, 8½ in. by 2⅞ in.,
no rings **0 10 0**

No. 2. Ditto, fitted with plated metal rings
at ends, head 9 in. by 3 in., weight
3 lb. 3 oz. **0 12 6**

These mallets should be carried in cases to prevent their
being soiled.   Price **4/6** each extra.

THE ROCKER MALLET.

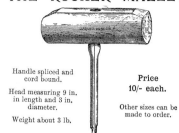

Handle spliced and cord bound.

Head measuring 9 in. in length and 3 in. diameter.

Weight about 3 lb.

Price 10/- each.

Other sizes can be made to order.

A new pattern, possessing all the advantages of a sliced mallet, and reducing the likelihood of taking the ground when striking, at same time lessening the weight slightly. A mallet shaped as this has also an extra advantage in playing balls adjacent to hoops.

THE ECLIPSE MALLET.

The feature of this mallet is that the head is sliced in a special way, which gives the sole an angle to the axis of the head. It is intended for the use of those adopting the front style of play.

PRICES.

General style exactly as in Association Patterns.

No. **1E.** Boxwood Head, 9 in. by 3 in. Weight 3 lb. 1 oz.
11/6

No. **2E.** Ditto head, 9¼ in. by 3⅛ in. Weight, 3 lb. 3 oz.
12/6

43   Three different mallets, from a Jaques catalogue of 1910. (*Courtesy Jaques and Son*)

10 WHERE TO PLAY

If you haven't got a big enough back garden, and even if you have, the best bet is to join a club. A club will give you a much better chance of improving your game because you will find yourself playing a greater variety of players than even the largest family or social circle can provide. If you want to start playing in tournaments, joining a club is more or less essential.

There are about 150 croquet clubs in Great Britain now, and the number is growing. Many of these clubs are funded at least in part by local councils and they are the product of the enthusiasm and voluntary hard work of their members. After all, the stars of the game are only the tip of the iceberg. Croquet owes its reputation and its existence to the mass of players who play it with enthusiasm rather than, necessarily, brilliance, and who play it more for fun than for glory. To get the address of a club near you, you need do no more than get in touch with the Croquet Association. You should write to:

The Administration Secretary
The Croquet Association
Hurlingham Club
Ranelagh Gardens
London SW6 3PR
Telephone 01 736 3148

Alternatively, it may be that you might wish to found a club yourself, and if that's the case, the Croquet Association will help you too. Contact:

The Development Officer
The Croquet Association
The Oaklands
Englesea Brook
Near Crewe
Cheshire SW2 5QW
Telephone 0270 820296

or care of the Croquet Association Office.

There is a variety of clubs to choose from. Some are new, some long established (the oldest is Worthing). Some are small, with only two or three courts; others have more. Southwick is the largest croquet club in the world in terms of courts, with eleven. The largest in terms of membership is Cheltenham. Some clubs offer croquet along with other sports, some offer only croquet. Some, like Hurlingham, are expensive, with sophisticated facilities and a long waiting list. Others are much less formal and only charge a nominal membership fee. Budleigh Salterton and Nottingham, two long-established clubs, are set in delightful surroundings.

At Hurlingham and Cheltenham, in equally lovely settings, the major tournaments are played. A 'centre of excellence' for croquet is under development at Kingston-upon-Thames – a new large club with seven full-size courts which, it is hoped, will be the first of a number of regional centres providing above-average facilities together with regular coaching sessions; and another new club is under way at Surbiton, which may well in the future become the CA's new headquarters.

In terms of more modest but equally valuable development, Bernard Neal points to what has been achieved at Nailsea near Bristol. This club was started in 1983. Sited in a public park, the condition of the ground originally was pretty unpromising: the grass was ragged and left uncut at three or four inches; the whole area was on a slope; the two courts each measured barely 15 yards and were equipped with little wire hoops. However, the club members knew what needed to be done and entirely by their own efforts have made great improvements. They are now embarking on a massive project to get the site levelled and extended to contain three full-size courts, raising the £12,000 needed, partly from the local council, partly from the Sports Council and partly from private collection. In general, a club will need at least two courts to be viable, because croquet is not space-effective: don't forget that a game on a full-size court can take three and a half hours

44   Nigel Aspinall winning the final of the Men's Championship, June 1983, Hurlingham. (*P L Alvey*)

and can usually only involve four people, at most, (but see double-banking, chapter seventeen, page 160).

Croquet players have their favourite courts. Nigel Aspinall enjoys playing at Hurlingham, Eastbourne and Colchester, 'because they're even-paced, smooth and flat', but doesn't like Southwick, and finds the courts at Cheltenham too hilly. 'Having to get used to an unfamiliar or disagreeable lawn is an irritant rather than a challenge but if one's playing in a competition one has to put up with it.'

Veronica Carlisle likes Hurlingham but enjoys Cheltenham too – 'because I've done well there,' and Hunstanton for nostalgic reasons:

> I know them and they're happy and they had bits here and holes there where the rabbits had been, and when the rabbits disappeared and the holes were there no longer it was sad!

She regrets too that at Hunstanton they've built up the corner of one court which once sloped down four inches or so and used to be fun to go and 'hide' in.

Some players have said that the Roehampton courts can be patchy and heavy going, and Keith Wylie, remembering that Colchester was once very fast and flat, feels that the courts there are not as good now as they once were, when Edward Duffield was in charge of them. Hurlingham was better before they introduced their automatic watering system in 1970 – and many players agree that the lush grass there is 'too perfect'. The automatic sprinkler system prevents the courts from drying out and thus becoming fast. Wylie finds them 'too easy' for his taste. John Solomon's favourite court is, however, precisely 'Number 4 at Hurlingham'. At Southwick, vibrations from passing trains nearby have been known to jiggle a still ball through a hoop! Fortunately, there is a Law to cover this contingency.

Do not worry if you have never held a mallet before if you feel you would like to have a go at croquet. The CA organise a number of 'come and try it' days, and a key part of the current development plan is the establishment of a national coaching network. Coaching sessions are sometimes included in the cost of joining a club, and in any case are very reasonable. The coaches are amateurs – do not forget that there are no croquet professionals – but they have participated in a coaching training scheme. A typical coaching package might consist of four or five two-hour lessons leading up to an explanation of and even an induction into the four-ball break, and including all the whys and wherefores of shot-making, basic strategy, and so on, for beginners; and there are follow-up courses for intermediate and even advanced players. Coaching sessions take place after work on weekdays and at weekends. Contact the CA for more information.

For younger would-be players, an increasing number of schools – among them the Royal Ballet School – and universities have croquet clubs, and it is hoped that croquet will be represented at the next World Games. Japan, Australia, Great Britain and the USA – if some agreement can be reached over the rules – are all likely participants.

At home, croquet is centred in England, with quite strong representation in Scotland, some in Ireland, and, at the time of writing, none in Wales. Useful addresses are given in Appendices B and C.

Tied in with the question, Where To Play? must be the question When To Play? It depends how keen you are. In Great Britain, the runs from late March to early October. Most players find that if their club is close by there is time for a game after work on a summer's evening, and if not, they play at weekends. Very enthusiastic players will use holiday time for croquet too – especially if they want to enter for one of the major tournaments which takes place over a week rather than a weekend. And don't forget that winners win just a trophy – which they take home for a year. Money prizes may not exceed £25. In 1986 Granada Television staged a short croquet tournament for a £150 'pot'. Aspinall won it, but £125 went back to the CA.

Croquet need not, however, be too demanding on one's time – especially if one plays it chiefly for recreation. Some practice is necessary, but less and less as one acquires one's eye for the game. By your second or third season you should need very little time to warm up, and then the amount of time you spend on the game will just be the amount of time you play in.

Apart from the growing number of croquet clubs, a number of hotels, which advertise regularly in *Croquet*, offer courts and equipment, and even croquet weekends. In 1986 the National Trust got together with Greene King, the brewers, and the Croquet Association to mount a series of exhibition games at stately homes across the country. So, who knows – perhaps country house croquet will return?

11 LAWN & EQUIPMENT CARE

LAWNS

> Should croquet enjoy the favour of the public yet a few years
> longer, we shall probably see artificial lawns under glass roofs,
> and balls made of some homogeneous substance,

wrote Prior in 1872. He was right about the balls, but the artificial
court has yet to make an impact on the world of croquet. It is true that
various types of artificial surface have been attempted, but players have
discovered a number of disadvantages. The balls tend to skid, or to be
pulled or pushed from their true course by the bias of the pile, or to
be nudged awry by the seams. Added to all of which there is the
question of cost. A full-size artificial court would be expensive: in the
region of £30,000.

John Solomon, with tantalising vagueness, remembers playing on
another type of surface

> at Naenae (in New Zealand), where we played on a bowling green
> which didn't have a blade of grass on it. It was rather like a clover
> with a shiny leaf which lay very flat on the surface. It was one of
> the finest lawns I have ever played on.

I have heard of play on camomile lawns, but would imagine the
going to be slightly spongy; and I cannot imagine a thyme lawn being
suitable. Added to which, such lawns would be slow to grow, and,
although requiring virtually no cutting, are a nightmare to weed. Only

the keenest croquet player suffering from appalling hay-fever should consider them!

That leaves us with grass, and if you are able and willing to have your own croquet court, what follows may be of value. Don't be daunted by the fact that a full-size court measures 35 yards by 28 – you can have a smaller one, provided it preserves the proportions of 5:4, and for family croquet any fair-sized patch of more-or-less tussock-free grass will do. Here I should like to insert a brief word about Edwin Budding, that unsung hero without whom no grass sports could have developed at all. In 1830, he adapted a machine which trimmed the pile on cloth in the factory where he worked in Stroud and invented the cylinder lawnmower. You can see one of the early models in the Lawn Tennis Museum at Wimbledon.

Richard Rothwell, a croquet player for over fifty years and a landscape-designer by profession, can be taken to speak with some authority on the subject of lawns. His own favourite courts – 'far and away the best in the world' – are those at Hurlingham, though he grants that they are rather on the slow side. This, as we have seen, is due to their automatic irrigation system. The lake at Hurlingham is below high-tide level on the Thames, which flows alongside the grounds. The groundsmen let water in through a sluice at high-tide, fill up the lake, and then pump it out through the irrigation system. The water is slightly saline, because at Putney the Thames is tidal.

The courts are basically laid with Cumberland turf. Being laid below river level, they were flooded by the river in 1928 (this was before the embankment that now exists was built) – you can still see a watermark a foot above the lintel of the main door of Hurlingham House which leads to the courts. The courts themselves were immersed in seven feet of water. When the water receded about two feet of silt was left behind, and on that base the present courts were laid.

Silt is the ideal subsoil for Cumberland turf, which grows naturally on sand, and drains well. It is therefore a wonderful playing surface, but it has been pampered at Hurlingham. Richard Rothwell remembers that just after the war the then head groundsman, Mr Graves, would lift each turf every other autumn and resettle it ready for the following year – an enormous job involving six under-groundsmen. But the practice helped to keep the ground aerated, and to combat compacting.

Rothwell's second favourite courts are those of the Gezira Club in Cairo – though I cannot say if they are still up to the standard they had in the early forties. At that time he would spend occasional leaves

45   Richard Rothwell, a player since 1936 and the Croquet Association's first full-time professional Secretary. (*Courtesy Richard Rothwell*)

there from the Western Desert, enjoying the company of such croquet 'greats' as Robert Tingey.

The Gezira Club was an amazing place. Constructed on an island, half-a-mile long by a quarter-of-a-mile wide, in the middle of the Nile, it had seven or eight squash courts – roofless because of the heat – a swimming pool, a golf-course, and a racecourse, as well as three croquet courts. These had trees planted round them for shade, and were sunken, rather like a bowling green or the front quad at Keble, Oxford. Every night after play had stopped the courts were flooded with river water, which by noon the following day, when play generally started again, had drained or evaporated away, leaving a perfect playing surface. The Nile silt provided a perfect subsoil for drainage, and the silt in the river-water (in those pre-Aswan dam days) added to it.

While we are abroad, I might add in passing that the most highly thought of American courts are at the Palm Beach Polo and Country Club in West Palm Beach, the Bon Vivant Country Club at Bourbonnais, Illinois, and the Meadow Club at Southampton, Long Island. The last is probably best of all, but membership is very far from cheap.

To return to Hurlingham (as our domestic Good Example). The courts are level – any defect is absolutely obvious, as for example the slight run-off in front of the first hoop on Lawn 3. At Hurlingham if you break down it will be your fault and not the fault of the court. The only disadvantage of that is that you have no-one but yourself to blame!

Talking, however, of unevennesses, you quite often find that you get dips in the jaws of hoops where the frequent passage of balls has scooped them out. The remedy is to move the hoop one hoop's width to the side to rest the worn piece of grass (this is within the 6-inch tolerance provided for in the Laws, but remember to shift all the hoops to the same side at the same time). Roll-offs can be a problem, too: Bernard Neal remembers a game which became completely bogged down because of a slope in front of the 4th hoop which made it impossible to run.

Are unevennesses more important factors than the type of grass used or the quality of the drainage? The two things are interrelated. An uneven lawn which nevertheless has thick, lush grass on it tends to have its unevennesses ironed out by the luxuriance of the grass. If the grass is short and burnished, the slightest surface defect comes to the fore, and at worst the surface can be so bumpy that it's all but unplayable. On the other hand, thick, long grass is slow, and it's harder to make the ball move across it – especially for any great distance. Grass should be cut low, and the lawn should be rolled frequently to keep it level. The ideal condition of a croquet lawn is for the grass to be slightly starved – though this will not look as pleasing as the lush greenness of a well-watered lawn; and remember that dry grass is fast grass. In the practically Saharan summer of 1976, Veronica Carlisle remembers, the balls at Hurlingham zoomed about like bullets at the merest touch.

It depends how fussy (or demanding) you are. Some people take the view that part of a player's skill should be in his ability to compensate for grass and surface irregularities. Most serious players, however, would agree that the lawn should be good enough to allow for perfect precision croquet. And if you are going to the trouble and expense of a lawn, you might as well have a good one:

> Whoever will play Croquet, must first see
> The Ground well chosen; and the Ground should be
> A Paradox wherein your sophists revel,
> At once a *lively* Ground, and a *dead* level.
> No undulating surface must be found,
> Where busy ants raise up their mighty mound
> So then to flatten every heap of mould,
> The grass-plat should diurnally be rolled.
>   (Anon. Printed in *Punch* 2 July 1864)

At Hurlingham, the lawns are mown every day of a tournament. For a domestic court, depending on how much use it gets, it would make sense to mow twice a week. Of course, to mow the lawn, you must remove the hoops, and the more frequently they are removed and replaced, the looser they become. This may be something you wish to bear in mind. Your choice of mower will be determined by the size of the lawn, but I think a cylinder mower is best – unless of course you actively dislike a 'striped' lawn.

Water according to your conscience, but take your lawn's ability to drain into account and don't drown it. For a domestic croquet lawn, avoid the purely compact grasses like Bents and Fescues because they won't take a lot of punishment. They are also slower growing, and require more care than the coarser Meadow and Ryegrasses, which are a good deal tougher. Probably the best bet will be predominantly Ryegrasses with some Bents and Fescues present. A smooth, even, and level surface is what you are predominantly aiming for. Roll monthly, or even fortnightly, and keep well aerated. Remove worm castes scrupulously, and pray that you are never invaded by moles!

Weeds should be discouraged but if you never get rid of them all do not despair, for no-one ever does. Most lawns will have at least a bit of clover, and a few daisies and dandelions. Keep weeds under control – especially the broad-leaved variety – and keep an eye out, too, for moss, which really should be seen off. If you are a tournament player, always make a note of the 'running' of the various courts you play: it can stand you in good stead. The late Humphrey Hicks, a *doyen* of the game and one of its foremost tacticians, often used his knowledge of the 'lie' of a court to his advantage.

The aesthetics of the surroundings of the court are a matter of personal taste. John Jaques II advises:

> On each side of the Croquet ground, a sloping embankment, rising 12 inches, should be made, and, for the convenience of spectators, this should be encompassed by a gravel walk 4 ft. wide. Beyond this walk, shrubs, vases, flowers etc., may be placed as the constructor may fancy.

I don't know about the need for a four-foot wide gravel walk, but an embankment is a good idea – or at least a clear area before any flowerbeds begin, as you will neither want to lose your croquet balls nor have them pick up dirt (croquet balls have a grooved surface).

One of the pleasantest lawns I have played on was sheltered from the wind by an old wall, covered with clematis à la Gertrude Jekyll, and flanked on one side by a stone terrace, which caught the afternoon sun, and where one could sit very pleasantly while waiting one's turn to play.

Instructions for lawn laying and siting are fully dealt with in James Dunbar Heath's *The Complete Croquet Player* of 1874, and take a lot of improving upon:

> The site selected for the ground should not be exposed to bleak winds, and yet, if possible, it should be high enough to afford a natural drainage. The subsoil on which the ground is made is of great importance – a gravelly or sandy substance being far better than clay. When, as in clayey soils, the natural drainage is not sufficient, the ground should be drained with unglozed [sic] earthenware pipes, laid at least 15 inches under the surface. They should be covered to a depth of about 3 inches with stones, potsherds etc., and the earth above well rammed down. In levelling the ground, made earth should be avoided as much as possible, as it is almost sure to settle unequally; therefore, if a site can be found that will require merely cutting away and removing, it should be preferred to one that will require an embankment to bring it to the proper level. If the subsoil be poor, the turf should not be placed directly on it, but on a layer of good earth some inches thick.

The best time for commencing operations is in September or October, though sometimes work is not begun until the Spring. Heath continues in great detail, concluding with advice on turf laying and dressing the ground:

> ...after two dressings of sand or sifted earth, the grass if poor, may then be dressed with fine leaf-mould to which a little guano or soot may be mixed with advantage.

Apart from the lawn, I think the most important elements are these: if possible, the court should be protected from the wind. Croquet doesn't require energetic movement, and a cold wind can reduce the enjoyment of players and spectators alike. Secondly, enough room for spectators or outplayers to sit comfortably, but not right on top of the court. A terrace would be ideal. Thirdly, comfortable seats to sit on. That is about all that is essential. Aesthetically, my own inclination would be to surround the lawn with trees and tall shrubs, to emphasise focus on it. But all this is the ideal – in practical terms, if you're setting up a small court in your own garden, just use whatever shelter you have available.

EQUIPMENT

Equipment care is not too much of a problem. Cast iron hoops may need rust removing, and repainting white at the start of the season. Wrought-iron hoops today are covered in a hard white plastic laminate and should need no maintenance. The base of the centre-peg may need an occasional lick of paint. All balls sold today (except some very cheap ones) are plastic or composition and need nothing more than a wipe clean every so often to get earth out of the grooving. If you have an old set of real boxwood balls, treat them with linseed oil to obviate splitting. Clips need almost no maintenance, but put a bit of Vaseline on the spring to prevent rust.

Your mallet, however, does deserve a bit of looking after. Wipe it clean and dry after every game or match and check the faces for splitting – this shouldn't happen but it might if you're a beginner, or play a lot, or both. On the whole, don't attempt repairs yourself if the head has split – Jaques do mallet repairs, as does Ken Townsend (address in Appendix A) – it's also possible that your club will have a member who can undertake repairs.

If you've leant the mallet against a wall for storage and the shaft has warped, turn it round and lean it the other way for the shaft to 'warp' back. Store your mallet head upright in a wall-clip if possible; if you can acquire an old croquet stand, so much the better (they are no longer made). Make sure the wood never gets too wet or too dry, and every so often give the mallet a light coat of yacht varnish. Brass-banded mallets look smart, and the brass bands are said to prevent chipping.

That is about all. If you read *Croquet* you will occasionally see articles on how to mend your shaft, and even how to make a mallet! My own feeling is that these matters are better left to experts, as I am not one, and I think money spent on an expert repair is money well spent.

46   A target, for outplayers or for practice. From a Jaques catalogue of 1931. (*Courtesy Jaques and Son*)

PART THREE

12 DRESS

DRESS

There is one article of dress which is essential: a pair of heel-less boots or shoes. Tennis shoes or trainers are the sort of thing to wear. Otherwise dress depends entirely on circumstances, although fashion and attitudes have changed down the years.

The Victorians – the ladies especially, but one suspects the gentlemen as well – used croquet as an excuse to dress up and show themselves off. Edwardians, if one may judge from the pictures that survive, seem to have been perfectly happy in ordinary street, country or golf clothes, and Duff Mathews would probably be asked to change if he could show up for a modern tournament in the clothes he wore in 1912. To be fair to him, the Croquet Association's Handbook for 1900 states positively that 'the game can be and *is* played (1) in almost all sorts of weather; (2) in almost all manner of attire'. However, Reckitt, who quotes this in his *Croquet Today* (1954) goes on to observe, gently, that 'though control of the weather is outside our powers, control of our attire is not'.

As late as 1955 Richard Rothwell ran into some trouble when he started wearing shorts – something of a pioneer activity in croquet then.

> I took to wearing shorts at tournaments to improve the image of the game – to show that it wasn't just a collection of old women of both sexes playing.

A year later, he was invited to play for the South of England against

Fig. 6. Grünes Lein=
wandkleid mit Säum=
chen und Steppnähten.

Fig. 7. Kleid aus erd=
beerrothem Leinenjtoff
oder Zephyr.

Neue Radfahr= und Tenniscoftüme.

47 Proof that the Germans knew nothing
about croquet. The caption reads 'new tennis
and cycling outfits'! (*Mary Evans Picture
Library*)

48 Dressed to croquet in the thirties. (*BBC Hulton
Picture Library*)

New Zealand. The Council's invitation included the minatory words
'subject to your wearing long white flannels'. Reckitt, offering general
advice at about the same time, is in line with this:

> With white flannels of course white shoes should be worn ... and
> if for any reason a man does not choose to play in white, he still
> cannot do better than play in flannel ... any other sort of cloth
> ... never looks quite right ... What looks inappropriate are
> shirtsleeves appearing from a waistcoat. If you are one of those
> who find it more comfortable to play in braces, get a light linen
> coat to wear over them in hot weather.

49   Very casual croquet in the twenties. The hoop, the condition of the lawn and the way she
is holding the mallet would make a serious player faint dead away. But what the hell! (*BBC
Hulton Picture Library*)

Turning to the ladies, at first he courteously leaves them to judge
for themselves, but then he goes on to be full of advice: avoid garden-
party dresses, he says, and

> wear sports clothes, preferably with a straight skirt without pleats
> which would impede play. [And] in cool weather a cardigan may
> be worn but not in violent colours which do not harmonize with
> the grass, the trees and the shadows of a croquet ground. Bright
> reds and oranges in particular are out of key here.

Reckitt, however, does not press the wearing of white for ladies, as he
points out with strenuous delicacy that 'the age at which many ladies
take up the game is not one at which a white costume is often most
flattering to them'. He ends with some very practical advice:

50   Dr Roger Wheeler is watched by referee Hugh Carlisle, QC, Hurlingham, 1978. (*P L Alvey*)

Always be sure that you have the means to keep warm ... at such tournaments as the Peel Memorials in May and Devonshire Park in October, the more massive your protection from the wind the happier you will feel – and when it is your turn, the better you will play.

Today, flannels have given way to man-made fibres, but a lot of what Reckitt says still holds good. Generally, men will wear a white sports shirt, short or long-sleeved, a white pullover if necessary, and white slacks or shorts. For women – despite what Reckitt says – the standard kit is very similar: white. Some like to play in shorts, but most seem to prefer slacks or a skirt cut wide enough to allow comfortable centre stance, and of a light enough material not to impede the mallet.

Finally, the weather. Croquet is not stopped by it – not by rain, hail or frost. The only thing that does stop it is standing water on the court. Real adepts may, therefore, want to go for over-all waterproofs, but I think that's a little extreme. Simply make sure that you have a good anorak, and that it's windproof, waterproof and ventilated. Also for play in wet weather, you will be happier with waterproof shoes, and perhaps a golf umbrella – that is if you have a partner or opponent who is willing to hold it over you while you are actually playing.

13 THE COURT AND
EQUIPMENT

THE COURT

'*Court*' is the term which is almost universally used nowadays, although '*lawn*', and '*ground*' may still be heard.

A full-sized croquet court measures 35 yards × 28 yards and is usually on grass. It can be a daunting prospect to the beginner approaching it for the first time, and 'hitting in' – ie making a long shot from one end of the court to the other – is not that easy and quickly disabuses people of the idea that croquet is a physically undemanding game. Indeed, in Australia beginners are only allowed to play on small courts and may not graduate to full-size croquet until they have achieve a certain handicap. For this reason short croquet may also prove a valuable introduction to the real thing.

The area is marked out by means of white lines on the grass, or by a tight string. These lines delineate the boundary and are the only markings.

Smaller courts may be used, provided the ratio of 5:4 is maintained, although I do not think that anything smaller than $17\frac{1}{2}$ yards by 14 yards would be very satisfactory for the 'real' game.

There is a permitted leeway of plus or minus 6 inches for all measurements relating to the court.

Short croquet is played on a court of slightly different proportions: 24 yards × 16 yards (3:2).

51   The perfect setting for the game – from John Jaques II's *Croquet*, 1864. (*Courtesy The British Library*)

One yard into the court from the boundary line is the *yard line*, which is not marked but which is traditionally located by using your mallet's length (standard $37\frac{1}{2}$ inches).

The area between the yard line and the boundary line is called the *yard line area*.

The four *boundary corners* are called *1, 2, 3, 4,* clockwise from bottom left. (Roman numerals are often used in diagrams to indicate them.) They may be marked by flags – blue, red, black, yellow, respectively. These flags are aesthetic rather than functional, and any one of them may be removed temporarily while you make a stroke if you find it is in your way.

A yard along each boundary line from the corner flag are set small white pegs. These are called *corner pegs*. Their purpose is to locate the corner spot, which is the unmarked intersection point on the court of the unmarked yard lines. As with the flags, they may be removed temporarily while you make a stroke.

The four sides of the court are known as *North* (between corners 2 and 3), then clockwise round *East, South, West,* although the court is not necessarily aligned to the correct points of the compass.

A 13-yard length on the yard line from corner spot 1 towards corner

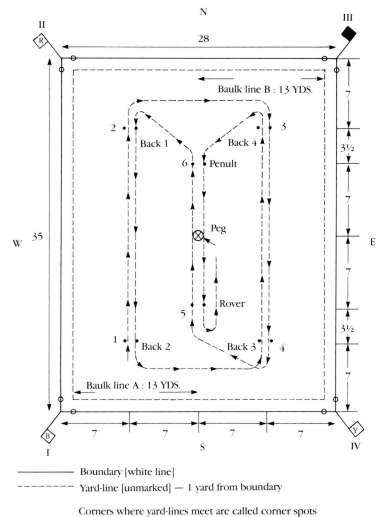

Boundary [white line]

Yard-line [unmarked] — 1 yard from boundary

Corners where yard-lines meet are called corner spots
Corner hoops [1,2,3,4] are 7 yards in from either side of boundary
Centre hoops [5,6] are 14 yards in from N.G.S boundaries and 10.5 yards in from E.G.U. boundaries
Starting hoop [1] has blue crown
Final hoop [Rover] has red crown
Arrows show direction of play [in US rules Rover is run in same direction as 5]

Fig. 1   Standard court and setting

spot 4 (ie half its length) and a similar length on the yard line from corner spot 3 towards corner spot 2 are called *Baulk lines A* and *B* respectively. It is from either of these that you play into the game.

In the centre of the court is the *peg*. This is nearly always wooden, although it may be metal or plastic, and is $1\frac{1}{2}$ inches in diameter and 18 inches high; it has a small detachable extension to which the clips can be affixed. The first 6 inches above the ground are painted white, and then it is painted in bands corresponding to the colours of the balls: yellow, black, red, blue.

The *hoops* are of metal and are painted white. The best quality ones are made of cast iron and have tapered spikes to keep them firm in the ground. This is important because it is easier to get a ball through a loose hoop than through a firmly fixed one.

A hoop should be 12 inches high above the ground, and there should only be $3\frac{3}{4}$ inches width for the ball to pass through, though for ordinary, friendly games 4 inches is still all right. For the very top tournament, the President's Cup, extra narrow hoops measuring only $3\frac{11}{16}$ inches wide are used.

The top of the hoop is called the *crown*, and the crown of the first hoop is painted blue and that of the last hoop is painted red. This is to enable anyone coming fresh to a croquet court to orientate himself immediately.

The side struts of the hoop are called the *wires*.

The four *outer* and *corner hoops* are located 7 yards in and along from the adjacent boundary lines.

The two *centre hoops* are located halfway along the North and South boundaries and $10\frac{1}{2}$ yards in from them.

Each hoop has two names, according to whether it is being run on the 'outward' or on the 'return' journey, as follows:

1 – 2-back
2 – 1-back
3 – 4-back
4 – 3-back
5 – rover
6 – penultimate

52   A good upper-end-of-the-market croquet set for the serious private player. (*Courtesy Jaques and Son*)

THE BALLS

We have come a long way from Lauthier, who, writing in the early eighteenth century about how to look after boxwood pall-mall balls, says: 'store them in a bag with dirty linen, which is the best place, being neither dry nor damp, to keep them sound'. In fact, it is impossible to buy wooden balls of any quality at all any more, though you will find some so-called 'boxwood' balls in the cheaper sets. Solid plastic balls are probably a better buy. Best quality balls are made of composition (high quality plastic over a cork core).

Correct *weight* is about 16 ounces.

Correct *size* is $3\frac{5}{8}$ inches in diameter, although you will come across smaller balls.

'Eclipse' balls, made by Jaques for tournament use, must have a rebound coefficient of between 27 and 33 inches when freely dropped from 60 inches onto a two-inch steel plate embedded in concrete, but they are not cheap.

CLIPS

Clips are just that, made of plastic or metal, and of colours corresponding to those of the balls. They are really used as an *aide-memoire*, and on the outward journey you put your ball's clip on the *crown* of the next hoop it's due to run, and on the return journey, you put it on the *wire* of the next hoop.

As we have seen, clips made rather a stir when Jaques first introduced them – it wasn't only Mayne Reid who disapproved of them. However, their use was vindicated when Walter Jones Whitmore and *The Field* came down in their favour.

THE MALLET

Although mallets don't come in quite the superabundance of designs that used to be seen, they are still the most personal and the most important item of the equipment. You may not be lucky enough to have a garden or a piece of land big enough to accommodate even a small croquet court, and in that case you needn't own a croquet set, but although clubs usually have a handful of old mallets for beginners to use while they are finding their feet, sooner or later you are going to want your own.

An important consideration is the *weight* of your mallet. This can vary from about 2 lb 10 oz to 3 lb 8 oz, but a good mean weight to aim for is 3 lb. Some players have a mallet made to a specific weight, and this can be done quite accurately by pairing up a head and a shaft.

A light mallet will facilitate stop-shots, but make long rolls harder. Lighter people should get a proportionately heavier mallet head and vice versa.

Never try to alter your mallet by cutting down the shaft or (even worse) the head, as you will destroy the mallet's balance and it will be ruined.

The *shaft* may be of wood or aluminium. Aluminium has a certain springiness, and also helps to bring the price down, but I find the material unsympathetic. Wood comes in various gradations. You can have a solid ash shaft, which has very little spring. A hickory shaft has more, and this can be increased by inserting a cane splice in the lower third section. The majority of serious mallets are made with such a shaft. If you wanted an even springier shaft, you could have it made of malacca, but you would have to get Jaques to make it for you specially, and although malacca was popular at the beginning of the century, most players today find it too whippy for properly controlled play.

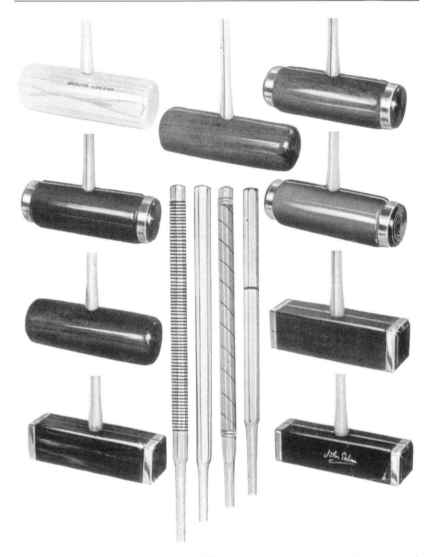

53   A selection of modern mallets showing different heads and grips. Brass-binding on the head helps prevent chipping. (*Courtesy Jaques and Son*)

A taller person may need a longer shaft, a shorter person or one who favours the Irish grip may need a shorter shaft, but the *standard height* from the top of the shaft to the bottom of the head is $37\frac{1}{2}$ inches.

Solomon believes that the shaft of a mallet is more important than its head, and the *Solomon mallet* – constructed to his design – features a solid hickory shaft with a $2\frac{1}{2} \times 2\frac{1}{4}$ inch square lignum head. Solid hickory is, as mentioned above, less springy than hickory with a cane splice, but it is much favoured in America. Jack Osborne plays with a Solomon mallet.

The *grip* around the shaft may be made of leather, cord, or rubber, or the wood may simply be corrugated on a lathe to give you a 'corrigrip' handle.

The *handle* may even be plain, but in that case it should be octagonal, except in standard, garden or junior sets.

The favoured wood for a mallet *head* is lignum vitae, from Central and northern South America, but supplies are dwindling, and alternatives are being sought. English ash is now in standard use. Alternatively, a mallet head need not be made of wood at all, but the laws specify that the material used must have no playing advantage over wood, and that the endfaces 'must be parallel and identical in every respect'.

The *endfaces* of a mallet head are round, though they may be square, or rounded with a flat bottom. The round endface is the most common, and the normal proportions of the complete mallet head are 9 inches long by 3 inches in diameter.

Round-headed mallets (as those with round endfaces are conveniently called) account for eighty percent of the market. The point about a round head is that you can get the requisite weight in a relatively inexpensive timber. A *square-headed mallet* is costlier because its cross-section measures only $2\frac{1}{2}$ or even $2\frac{1}{4}$ inches, and to get the same weight you need to use a hardwood with a sufficiently high specific gravity.

The most uncommon form of mallet has a *round head with a flat base*, which is sometimes covered with a brass sole-plate to make up the weight. It is called a *Peel mallet* after Walter Peel, who designed it, and it can be made to order by Jaques. It is not cheap and its advantages are perhaps hard to see, although if you lay it down – say to measure the yard line – you can roll it upright again with your foot without stooping! Also, of course you can stand it up on its own like a square mallet.

Bernard Neal assembles and markets a relatively inexpensive mallet (though it also comes in a de luxe version) for the Croquet Association. Its square head is made of 'Permali' – compressed laminated beechwood which was in fact created as a commercial substitute for lignum, and for which the principal industrial use is in electrical transformers. Walker Croquet Equipment cut and shape the head for him.

Walker Croquet Equipment also market an unusual mallet with a head made of a white plastic called 'Duralon'.

Finally, Jaques do a complete boxed set with square-headed mallets at the top of their range, although the tendency is for serious players to buy their own individual mallets.

The relative merits of the various mallet heads

Does a square-headed mallet have any advantage over a round one? Certainly a square-headed mallet is convenient when you want to use it to line balls up: it will freestand on the court and serve as a marker. It's convenient, too, to be able to leave it freestanding upright when the grass is wet – for that way the handle remains dry. Also, if you slightly mishit on the bottom of the mallet a flat bottom means that the course of the ball isn't affected. And flat sides are an advantage if you have to play a shot in which your mallet is hampered by the proximity of a hoop: you still have the whole face of the mallet to hit with.

Having said all that, most players will tell you that effectively there is no difference of any significance, and you will find that people tend to play with the shape of head they started with and have got used to. Nigel Aspinall has experimented with a square-headed mallet but until recently generally preferred the old round one he had always played with. Eric Solomon (no relation to John) once played with an outsize square mallet, painted entirely red.

A mallet can become quite a personal thing, an extension of oneself, so that how well you play can have as much to do with how comfortable you feel with your mallet as with any physical advantage of the mallet itself. Well-cared for, a mallet should last forever. It requires little maintenance and you should only ever need one for personal use (though keep a spare if you play a lot in case of accidents). You're not allowed to change your mallet during a turn unless it breaks, and you will rarely see a player arrive at a croquet court with a clutch of mallets, as a tennis player may with his armful of racquets! If you are going to play seriously, it is worth noting that the majority of players who do, nowadays use a square-headed mallet.

14 THE GAME

Whole books have been written about how to play croquet, and I must stress that in this chapter I am not endeavouring to do more than cover some of the basic principles. This is primarily for the reader who has not yet played the game, or for the beginner who feels that there is still much to be understood. *The Basic Laws* appear in Appendix E, and most croquet sets from reputable manufacturers come with a copy of either the *Full* or the *Basic Laws*. There are variations in the Laws for Advanced and Semi-Advanced play, for players with a low or minus handicap, thus creating 'two nations' in croquet – Advanced Laws players and ordinary players – though there are indications that in the future this differentiation may be done away with.

In fact the Laws of croquet are being polished and refined and talked over more or less all the time; since 1960 they have been redrafted twice – although most of the changes are fine tuning.

However, in the years between the wars some significant changes were introduced to the rules of the game. The top of the first hoop had been painted blue in 1904, and in 1924 it was decided to paint the top of the last hoop red, but these were minor innovations, simply intended to help players orientate themselves on the court. Far more importantly, in 1922 the setting we know today, of six hoops and *one* peg, was finalised. It is called the Willis setting after its inventor, C E Willis. It was introduced because it was more difficult than the Hale setting, in which it was possible for a skilled player to send his ball through two hoops and peg out in one stroke.

The other important change was the introduction in 1920 of the so-called 'either ball' game – hitherto players had been obliged to play the balls invariably in the colour sequence blue-red-black-yellow. Now, the player playing blue and black or red and yellow could play whichever ball he chose in his turn (with the exception of the first four turns of the game which must get all the balls into play). Modern players reading books on croquet written before 1920 should therefore be on their guard – many of the tactics will not make sense! In fact, still today, you will occasionally find families who play the pre-1920 game: balls played in sequence, and the old Hale 2-peg setting. And if you play in the USA, the sequence game is *officially* retained.

Sometimes the laws have become so intricate that they have caught themselves out, but a beginner should not be daunted by them. The laws that cover what to do are simple and clear – the rest of them have been drawn up to try to cover what happens in the multiplicity of different situations that can occur in a game, and if you learn them as you go along, they will not seem so difficult. Describing the rules of any game in a book makes them sound forbidding, but put into practice they aren't that bad at all.

The game is normally played by two or four players. Four players play in pairs, and each player takes one ball.

The balls are always played blue and black against red and yellow.

The game starts with all the balls being played into the game in sequence in the first four turns: blue, red, black, yellow. You can always remember this sequence because the peg is painted in these colours in bands, in descending order. You can play into the game from either baulk-line.

Once all the balls are in play, either ball can be played in a turn. When a turn ends, the other side takes over.

You cannot change the colour ball you are playing during a turn.

You cannot change your mallet during a turn, unless it breaks.

The object of the game is to go through all the hoops in the order shown on page 119, and to hit the peg with both balls of a side. The side that achieves this first wins.

John Solomon has described croquet as 'nothing more than a state of mind, given that you've done the hard work of learning how to play the strokes so that they come virtually automatically'. I can do no more than try to set you on the right path. The most important general things

54 Side style, or stance.   55 Hoop running.

to remember are to adopt the style which is most comfortable to you, and to make the first shot of every innings count.

STYLE

You have a choice of *side style* or *centre style*. In the first your body is facing the target at which you are aiming the ball but the mallet is swung to the side of your legs. In centre style the mallet is swung between your legs. Side style is quite rare today, and unless you particularly wish to adopt it I would opt for centre style. In this the weight of the body is equally balanced on the feet, which are placed wide enough apartow a pendulum-like swing of the mallet between them. I think it is best if one foot is placed slightly in front of the other, for better balance. Style is also called 'stance'.

56 Standard grip, US version, front view.   57 Standard grip, US version, side view.

GRIP

There are various ways of holding the mallet, and strictly speaking there is no 'wrong' way. The best plan is to start with the *standard grip*, and if you do not feel comfortable with that, experiment with some of the others. Or you may find, as I did, that your hands take hold of the mallet handle all by themselves in the way that is most comfortable to them. I found that they adopted what I had imagined when I first saw it would be the most unmanageable grip of all – the *Irish grip*. The *Solomon grip* has a significant following. Aspinall uses the Irish grip, Bernard Neal the *British standard grip*. Notice in this that the index finger of the right hand is extended down the shaft. It was not ever thus. A rule-book for 1907 complains:

> the mallet must be held in two hands, so that there can be no division into hostile camps of one handed and two handed players as of yore; nor, considering the weight to be supported, is it easy to hold them in the namby pamby way adopted by most ladies and some men, with the forefinger pointed down the handle.

All the grip illustrations, incidentally, show a right-handed player. Left-handed players should simply reverse the hand positions.

58   Standard grip, British version, front view.

59   Standard grip, British version, side view

60   Solomon grip, front view

61   Solomon grip, side view

62 Irish grip, front view   63 Irish grip, side view

STALKING

This is most important, as a prelude to hitting your ball (it's called the *striker's ball* while it's in play with you playing it). Lord Tollemache said hitting your own ball properly was the hardest thing to do and he was right – it's worth practising as it's very important.

The action of hitting the ball is the culmination of getting a number of other factors – body and mind co-ordination and timing – perfectly right before doing so. Don't be daunted by this, but do be patient, or you will never get it right. Get a little distance away from the striker's ball and then walk towards it in line with your direction of aim, with your mallet head pointing at it. Look at where you want to send the striker's ball, and then down at the ball itself, at the precise part of it that you intend to hit. Take up your position. Swing the mallet slowly back and, never taking your eye from your ball, hit it smack with the mallet head's face when the mallet head is parallel to the ground; don't stop there but follow the stroke through until the mallet has completed its natural swing forward, and do not look up or anywhere else until the entire movement is over. At all times the arms and the mallet should be acting as one and the arms, hands and wrists in unison should be controlling the mallet. The rest of the body should not interfere, but simply provide a comfortable, solid base for them to operate from. That is the basic stroke, but there is of course a variety of shots, which I shall outline in the following section.

THE SHOTS

Single-ball shots

These are:
1 the roquet;
2 the rush: (a) the straight rush, (b) the cut rush, (c) the long rush;
3 running the hoop;
4 the jump shot;
5 the hammer shot.

1 The roquet

For this shot you hit your own ball with the mallet, aiming at another ball. If you hit that other ball with your ball, you've made a roquet. This is a corner-stone shot, for if you pull it off you can get a croquet stroke, and after that a continuation shot. Of course, if you miss the other ball, then that is the end of your turn.

So, line up for the shot as I have already described, stalking your striker's ball; but at the beginning of your stalk, draw a bead on an imaginary line connecting you, your ball, and the ball to be hit (the *object ball*). Solomon describes his approach to such a shot, when the ball to be hit is a long way off, say 18–20 yards: 'on a number of occasions to my eye that ball has become as big as a football, and I have *known* I was going to hit it' – that is precisely the level of concentration and the positive attitude of mind you must aspire to. Provided that you carry the swing through as described above, and that your stance is aligned to the direction of aim, you should be able to develop this stroke quite quickly – but don't rush anything, and best of all, get some coaching.

2 The rush

This is a roquet in which you send the object ball where you want it to go, or at least in a predetermined general direction.
(a) *The straight rush* sends both the striker's ball and the object ball directly forwards.
(b) *The cut rush* sends the object ball off at an angle (which you can

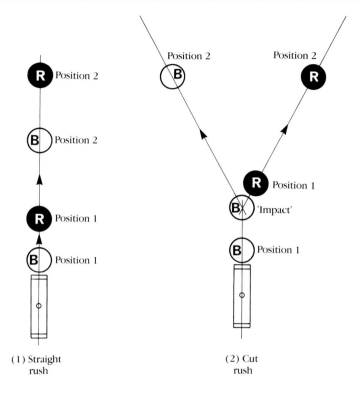

Fig. 2   Two sorts of rush

determine). This stroke is made by sending your ball to hit the object ball on its left side to send it to the right, and vice versa.

(c) *The long rush:* one important thing about a rush is that to be fairly sure of success you should not attempt one unless the two balls involved are less than a yard apart. More than a yard makes the gambit a *long rush*, which can be a pretty hairy undertaking.

Don't forget that whichever of the above shots you are playing it doesn't matter where the striker's ball goes, since you are going to pick it up and place it next to the object ball to take croquet from it after the successfully completed stroke anyway. (This is only true up to a point; under certain circumstances it can in fact matter.)

3 Running the hoop

This simply means sending your ball through the hoop. You often see people who've been playing as smooth as silk come to a dead easy hoop shot and botch it. You, and they, can't believe it, but there the ball lies,

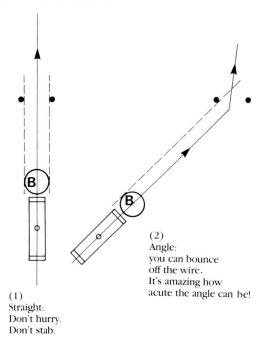

(1)
Straight:
Don't hurry.
Don't stab.

(2)
Angle:
you can bounce
off the wire.
It's amazing how
acute the angle can be!

Fig. 3 Running a hoop

jammed in the jaws of the hoop or bounced off one of its wires. Why? Perhaps because there's nothing to aim at but an empty space, and you know you've only got about $\frac{1}{8}$ inch clearance to get through. Perhaps, too, because running a hoop is *progress*, and that alone is enough to make you nervous. The thing to do is simply *not* to get nervous, but to line up for the shot as you would for any other single-ball shot. Don't hit the ball too gently, and don't try to stab it through the hoop as if you could whack it through by main force. Remember to complete the swing. If you've lined up correctly, the ball will do its job and the hoop will seem less like a strait gate than a triumphal arch! As you get better, you will be amazed at the acuteness of angle from which a hoop can be run, and you will learn other things like getting the ball through by bouncing it off one of the wires in a jump shot.

4 The jump shot

For this shot you stand right over the ball to be hit, hold the shaft of the mallet towards the centre, and hit down sharply on the ball – which instead of being driven into the earth as you might suppose, jumps up and forwards. Only practice will help you control how high or how far.

I wouldn't attempt this shot right at the beginning, but it's useful when you want to get to the other side of something that's in your way – whether it's a ball, another hoop, or even (on occasion) the peg. In fact, it's not all that hard to pull off, and – if you avoid ramming the head of your mallet into the lawn at the end of the stroke – looks impressive.

5 The hammer shot
For this shot you stand with your back to the object ball and bring the mallet down hammer-like on to the striker's ball. It is only for use *in extremis*, when the physical surroundings inhibit the normal swing.

Basic double-ball shots

These are:
1 the drive;
2 the stop shot;
3 the roll;
4 the take-off;
5 the split shot;
6 the cannon.

Once you have made your roquet successfully, you are ready to take croquet. This is the shot which makes the game what it is, that encapsulates its charm, and so it is not surprising that the croquet stroke has a number of variations, and indeed variations on variations. Only the six most common are mentioned here.

1 The drive
This is the basic croquet stroke, and it is the only one where your stance and swing are the same as for the roquet stroke. The length of the drive depends on the power you want to put behind it, but in any case the object is to send both balls straight forward: the croqueted ball will travel two-thirds farther than the striker's ball.

2 The stop shot
The objective here is to send the croqueted ball much further than the striker's ball. To achieve it, stand a few inches further back from the striker's ball than you normally would, and when you strike it ensure

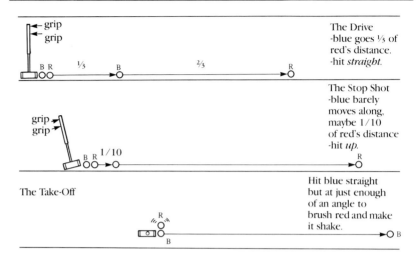

The Drive
-blue goes ⅓ of red's distance.
-hit *straight*.

The Stop Shot
-blue barely moves along, maybe 1/10 of red's distance
-hit *up*.

Hit blue straight but at just enough of an angle to brush red and make it shake.

The Take-Off

Fig. 4   Three croquet strokes. In the stop shot don't follow through. Sink the back of the mallet head to the ground after impact.

that the face of your mallet is hitting up at it. Do not follow through, but after impact drop the back of your mallet head into the ground. Keep a loose grip, too.

3 *The roll*

The roll has various forms, but essentially it is designed to have the opposite effect to the stop shot – that is, to send the striker's ball as far as the croqueted ball, or almost as far, or even further, when it is called a *pass-roll*. In a *half-roll* the striker's ball goes half the distance of the croqueted ball. In a *full-roll*, the distance travelled is near-enough equal. Bernard Neal explains:

> in a roquet and a croquet stroke if you hit down on your ball you impart a forward spin to it, and if you don't, you don't spin it – and that makes a difference to how far the ball will go. In an extreme case imagine two balls lined straight ahead for the croquet stroke – by hitting very sharply down you can make your ball go past the croqueted ball – up to twice as far past. In the pass-roll, just after mallet-impact, your ball is spinning fully, but the croqueted ball is simply sliding along the grass, and by the time it picks up spin so that it's properly rolling, that of course slows it down, and there's a fairly simple calculation you can do which shows that you can get legitimately, without 'pushing' your ball

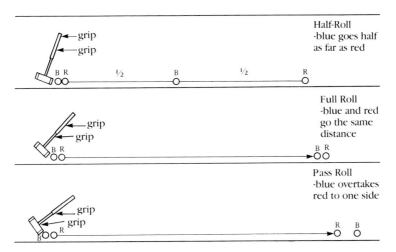

Fig. 5   Three rolls. In each of these shots you are hitting down on the ball. Note the angle of the mallet. The Pass Roll is a very difficult shot. Hit down *sharply*. Don't touch the mallet head.

past, a ratio of 49:25 – as near as damn it 2:1 – the extreme pass roll.

The more extreme you wish the roll to be the lower your grip must be down the mallet shaft, and necessarily you play side style, not centre style, as you crouch for the shot. Always remember, however, that you may not touch the head of the mallet – that is a fault. Some mallets come equipped with a shallot-shaped 'roll grip' near the head.

4 The take-off

This shot is rather more straightforward. The Laws provide that the croqueted ball need not be moved, but it must at least be 'shaken'. You may find yourself in a situation (it happens quite frequently) where you want to send your ball off to some other point on the lawn, but to leave the croqueted ball where it is. To satisfy the Laws you therefore 'take off' from the croqueted ball. You set the balls up and line your ball up for the direction you want it to go, just angling it in to the croqueted ball to brush it as you pass. This, in fact, is an extreme split-shot.

5 The split shot

There is an infinite variety of split shots, but basically it is a croquet stroke played at an angle. This time, however, unlike the cut rush, we care about where both balls end up.

This particular shot has been the occasion of much debate since John Solomon wrote an article in *Croquet* for April 1960 under the pseudonym 'J.U.U.S.', in which he argues that the correct direction to hit in is towards a point bisecting the line drawn between the two projected destinations of the balls, rather than (as had hitherto been argued) bisecting the angle of their proposed lines of travel. For those

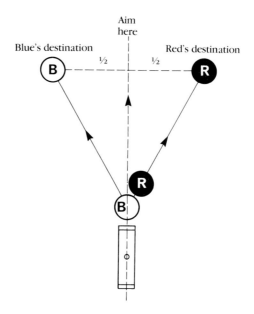

Aim halfway between the destinations you've chosen for the balls.

Fig. 6   A simple split shot.

interested, Solomon's view, now generally held to be correct (indeed, it is easily provable), is taken up with enthusiasm and at length in David Miller and Rupert Thorp's *Croquet and How to Play It*. They in turn recommend an article in *Engineering* for June 1962 by C R Calladine and Jacques Heyman called 'The Mechanics of the Game of Croquet' – and in the summer of 1980 F Fraser Ross constructed a croquet machine to test the theories 'J.U.U.S.' had advanced twenty years earlier. You can see how obsessive the game can be.

6 Cannoning

This is also permitted in croquet, and thus situations occur where you croquet and make a roquet in the same stroke.

THE SEQUENCE

1 A turn may consist of a single stroke.
2 When all the balls are in play (ie no balls have yet pegged out) either ball can be played in a turn, but you cannot change the ball you are playing in a turn.
3 Extra strokes follow:
  (a) making a roquet – the obligatory stroke following this is 'taking croquet';
  (b) taking croquet; ⎫ the strokes following these are called
  (c) running a hoop; ⎭ 'continuation strokes'.

After *running a hoop* you may use the continuation stroke to make roquet if you wish. A ball is deemed to have run its hoop if, when having entered the jaws of the hoop from its playing side, it has so far passed through them that it cannot be touched by a straight edge placed against that side of the hoop.

After *taking croquet* you may use the continuation stroke to roquet another ball.

After running a hoop you may roquet and croquet each of the other three balls in this manner once each only. Then you must run your next hoop. If you fail to do so your turn ends. However, if you do run your next hoop the whole sequence may start again.

In the roquet stroke, the turn does *not* end if either ball goes off the court. The roqueted ball is replaced on the yard-line nearest to the point it went off and croquet is taken from there. The striker's ball would simply be placed to take croquet, if it had gone off court.

Continuation strokes are never cumulative. If you run your hoop and in the same stroke make a roquet, you then take croquet immediately. You don't get the continuation stroke you would otherwise have earned by running the hoop. Similarly, if you make a roquet in a croquet stroke, you immediately take croquet and then play the continuation stroke.

If you neither run a hoop nor hit another ball your turn ends.

If you croquet off court, your turn ends. A ball is off court if any part of it touches the inside edge of the boundary line. A ball off court must be replaced on the yard line adjacent to the point where it went off.

You may deliberately wish to end your turn – in order, for example, to play your other ball, but always try to end a turn leaving the balls to the least advantage to the other side, and to the most potential advantage to your side, if possible.

4 When your turn comes round again, you may play whichever of your two balls you choose, and you may roquet and take croquet all over again, even if you haven't run your hoop yet after roqueting and croqueting all three balls in your last turn. Each new turn is a fresh start.

5 *Pegging out:* Once one of your balls has run the last hoop it is known as a *rover* and is 'for the peg', but it is advisable not to peg out immediately but to use the rover ball in a break (see page 144) to help your other ball round (or your partner's ball in doubles).

Only a rover ball can peg out another rover ball. If any other ball hits the peg, nothing happens.

If there are two rover balls of opposing sides it will usually be to your advantage to try to peg out your opponent's rover in a croquet stroke, thus disadvantaging him for the rest of the game by putting him one ball down.

If both your balls are rovers, be very careful in pegging out. The sequence is: roquet; croquet to peg out object ball; peg out striker's ball with continuation stroke.

If you peg out the object ball on the roquet stroke, you cannot then take croquet from it, because it is pegged out – out of the game. Your turn therefore ends, leaving your remaining ball on the court and at the mercy of your opponent. Many games have been lost like this, when all but won.

A three-ball game is one which is still continuing, when one of the four balls has been pegged out.

A two-ball game is one which is still continuing, when one ball of each side has been pegged out.

SCORING

Each hoop run counts 1 point for each ball, and the peg counts as 1 point. Thus each ball scores a total of 13 points, and the total possible score for a player is 26.

Scores are recorded in a slightly complicated way. If you have scored 26 and they have scored 4, you win by the difference, ie by $+22$, and they lose -22. It is not infrequent in top-class croquet to see wide-margin wins, for the better the players, the less likelihood there will be of them losing their innings, and thus the fewer turns there will be in a game.

FAULTS

This is the term given to fouls, and if one is committed and not waived or condoned by the opponent, the balls are replaced in the positions they were in before the stroke in which the fault was committed was played and the turn ends. The commonest faults are these:

— touching the head of the mallet with your hand (during a roll-stroke);

— double-tapping (not hitting the striker's ball cleanly with the mallet);

— shepherding, or pushing the struck ball along with the mallet (the Victorians called this 'spooning');

— 'crushing' the ball between the mallet and either the wires of a hoop or the peg;

— failing to shake or move the croqueted ball in the croquet stroke.

Section D of Part 2 of The Laws deals with 'Errors and Inter-ference With Play' in general.

Each player is his own referee, and may ask his opponent questions about the state of the game at all times. But although the striker is his own judge with regard to faults, if he fails to notice an error which he has committed his opponent may remark on it. He may even call for an official referee to watch the game for a time. On the other hand, opponents are perfectly at liberty to consult with one another over a questionable stroke.

In general, the striker must not be in any way pestered during his turn by the opponent, but in an honest difference of opinion, the striker should defer to the judgement of the other. Or, by mutual consent, an informed, disinterested spectator can be consulted. In serious or tournament play, the outplayer should not be on the court at all, and the only advice that a player may accept is from his partner in doubles play.

15 TACTICS AND PRACTICE

THE OPENING

There are various openings possible to a game of croquet, but I am going to deal only with the most common. In any case, a coin is tossed before play starts, as in a lot of other games. There the resemblance ends, for the winner of the toss now has a choice: he can elect to play first, or to put his opponent in first, *or* he can choose what colour balls he wants to play with. The reason for this is not known: it may be a throwback to the time when the balls were played strictly in colour sequence, or it may have had something to do with the early days when one pair of balls may actually have been better than another. Some players even confess to a superstitious need to play with balls of a certain colour; I personally prefer to play with black and blue if I possibly can. My advice to a toss-winner is to opt for the choice of lead, because it seems daft to hand over such a powerful choice to one's opponent. There are many, however, who feel that going in first or second is of no significance in croquet, and that that is the real reason why the toss is so eccentric.

At any rate, he who has first go plays his first ball in – it doesn't matter which, and he can do so from baulk line A or B.

The obvious thing to do is aim for the first hoop. But this isn't advisable because if you fail to run it (all too likely from 6 yards) but get near it, you've left a ball conveniently at a hoop for your opponent to make use of. Now, one of the most important things in croquet is to think hard, think ahead, and consider every possibility. As Solomon says:

Whenever you take a shot ... you must think where the balls will be at the end of the stroke if you should miss and therefore what chance that will give to your opponent. Not: "What do I gain if I hit?" but "*What do I give away if I miss?*"

The strategy of the standard opening is so well-known to croquet players that it must seem as ritualised as the standard chess openings, but if it wasn't the best way to start it would have been abandoned by now. For those interested, I recommend the article on Openings in Keith Wylie's *Expert Croquet Tactics*, with the caveat that it is a highly technical book, and not for the uninitiated.

Let's say that blue and black are first to play. Blue goes to Corner 4. Red and yellow are to play now (for the first four turns of a game are played sequentially to get all the balls into play). Red plays some way up the west boundary to come to rest somewhere to the west of hoop 1. Both these balls have been played from baulk line A, by the way, as are all the balls in this opening. The reason red has been put there is to tempt black to shoot at it; but as red is 10 yards from the baulk line it's not an easy target to hit, and if black misses he will be disadvantageously placed, because yellow may then be able to shoot at

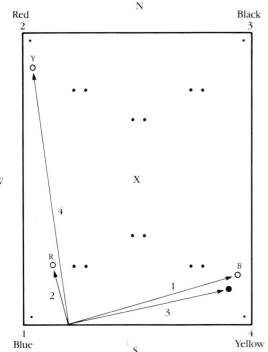

Fig. 7 An opening: Black did not take Red's tice; Yellow has tried to roquet Red and missed, but gone on towards the 2nd corner.

him and red, and, hitting one of them, quickly use them to establish a 'break' (see more, below). Red is said to have offered a 'tice' ('enticement') to black. If black does go for it, he should hit hard enough to be carried well past, up towards corner 2, out of harm's way, if he misses. If he doesn't, he should join blue in corner 4. Let us assume he does this. Yellow has now to play in. He aims to hit red, but hits hard enough to go all the way up to corner 2 if he misses – again, out of harm's way. Remember always: *'what do I give away if I miss?'* Leaving yellow near red would give black and blue too good a chance to hit one of them and establish a break.

The game is now opened, and it is blue and black's turn to play (for simplicity, I am assuming that no roquets have been made), and it can be whichever of the two balls their player chooses to use – though he must, of course, *continue to play the same ball for the duration of this turn.* In all probability, he will shoot at red or yellow with one of them, and attempt to establish a break.

BREAKS

These form the backbone of the game. Basically the striker's ball uses the other balls on the court to help him get around the hoops. 'All the balls are grey when you're playing with them,' says Aspinall. 'It is only at the end of the turn that their colour has any significance.' Until then they are all equally useful to your purpose of getting your ball through its hoops in order.

There are three kinds of break: the two-ball break; the three-ball break; and the four-ball break.

In the two-ball break the striker's ball has one other ball to help it. This is the easiest type of break to 'pick up' (get started) but the hardest to maintain, because it involves a lot of long shots. Correct positioning of the two balls involved is crucial. The object ball is kept ahead of the striker's ball and needs to be accurately rushed every time to where you want it. On the croquet stroke, the split shot comes into its own.

In the three-ball break, your ball has two other balls to help it, and these two are arranged so that one is near the hoop you have to run next (the 'pilot' ball), and the other near your next hoop but one (the 'pioneer' ball). Always, once you have used the pilot to run your hoop, send him on to the next hoop but one, to become the new

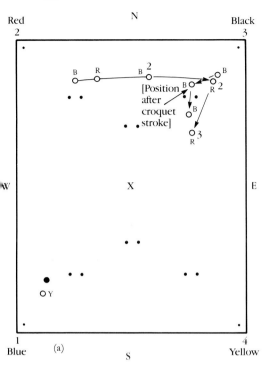

Fig. 8 **2-ball break**

(a) Blue rushes Red to Position 2;
Blue croquets Red to 3, and splits
to in front of hoop;
Blue runs hoop on continuation
shot.

(b) Blue rushes Red to Position 2;
Blue croquets to position 3 Red
and splits to in front of hoop;
Blue runs hoop on continuation
shot.

(c) Blue gently roquets Red and the
croquets it to Position 2, splitting
itself to in front of hoop;
Blue runs hoop in the
continuation stroke;
The sequence continues.

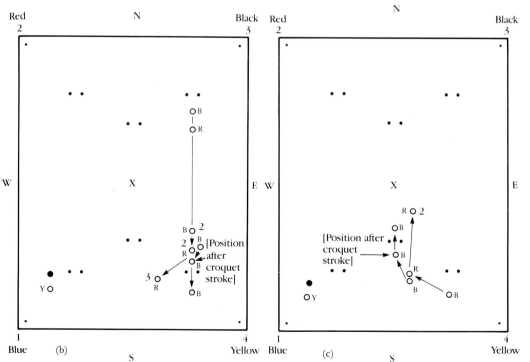

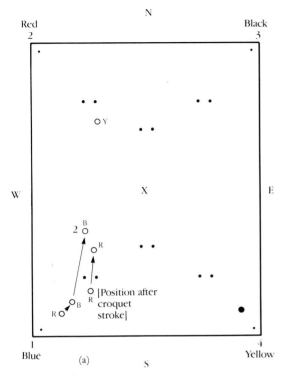

Fig. 9 **3-ball break**

(a) Red gently roquets Blue and then croquets it
    to Position 2, splitting to in front of the hoop;
    Red runs the hoop on the continuation stroke.

(b) Red rushes Blue to 2, and croquets it to 3;
    With its continuation shot, Red roquets
    Yellow and croquets it to 2, splitting to in
    front of the hoop;
    Red runs the hoop with its continuation shot.

(c) Red rushes Yellow to 2, and in the croquet
    stroke sends Yellow to 3, splitting to behind
    Blue;
    The sequence then recommences.

A 3-ball break is a 4-ball break without the pilot.
It involves some pretty difficult shots.

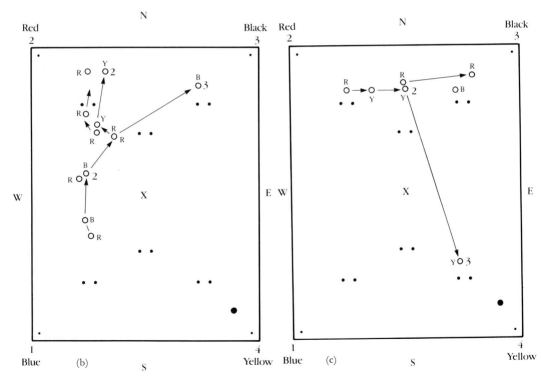

pioneer. The advantage of having two balls to help you is that there is less risk of 'breaking down' (losing your turn) than there is with only one helper ball. The *problem* with the three-ball break is that it requires even greater concentration – you have to be fully aware of what you are doing, and what you are going to do in the next few strokes, all the time. However, if you do not forget the basic sequence of roquet–croquet–continuation, and if you practise the break on your own, you should find that once you are into the rhythm it will play itself. Be patient.

The four-ball break uses all three other balls on the court to help the striker's ball. It's that much easier to maintain than the three-ball break, but it will seem a little confusing at first because instead of making straight for the next hoop, you make various detours around the court in order to set up the helper balls for the following hoops, and to do this involves what appears to be a form of leap-frogging. Of course, you may not find it confusing at all. Bernard Neal tells the story of Paul Hands, now a top player, who, as a beginner, was shown a four-ball break. When asked shortly afterwards if he understood its principle, he replied with unconscious perceptiveness: 'But how could

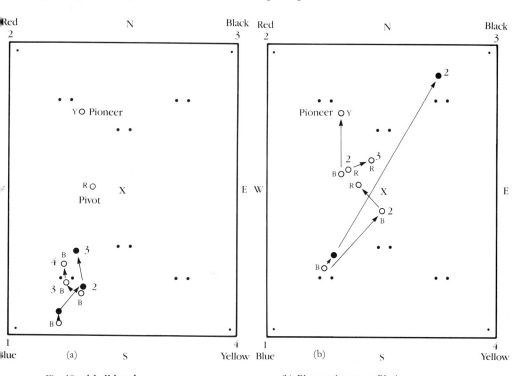

Fig. 10 **4-ball break**

(a) Blue rushes Black to Position 2;
  Blue croquets Black to 3 and splits to its
  Position 3;
  Blue runs the hoop with continuation shot and
  ends up at 4.

(b) Blue *gently* roquets Black;
  Blue croquets Black to 2 and splits to its
  position 2;
  Blue *gently* roquets Red with its continuation
  shot;
  Blue croquets Red to its position 3 and takes
  off to Yellow.

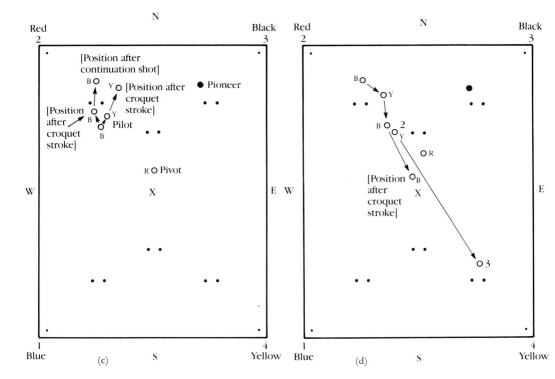

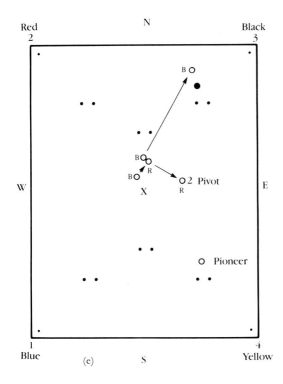

Fig. 10 (continued)

(c) With its continuation shot, Blue roquets and
    then croquets Yellow to the other side of the
    hoop;
    Blue runs the hoop with its continuation shot.

(d) Blue roquets Yellow to 2 and in the croquet
    stroke sends it to 3, itself splitting to below
    Red.

(e) Blue gently roquets Red and takes croquet from
    it, splitting it to 2 and itself to behind Black,
    ready to recommence the sequence.

Remember – successful breaks depend on accurate
ball-placing.

you play it any other way?' On the other hand, Keith Wylie, a man of great intellect, admits that he had to be shown a four-ball break in action before he could begin to understand it.

Again, however, once the logic of what is being done has been grasped, all becomes clear and the break, once picked up, can be a sure-fire way of getting you all the way round without breaking down. In addition to the pilot and pioneer of the three-ball break, the third helper ball is introduced at a point somewhere midway between the hoop you have to run and your next hoop but one. This ball is called the 'pivot' ball and it provides you with a constant stepping stone between pilot and pioneer, thus reducing risk still further. The more expert a player is, the fewer risks he will take, unless through error he is forced to take them.

Merlin Karlock, President of the Bon Vivant Country Club in Bourbonnais, Illinois, has accurately described the game as '60% strategy, 30% skill and 10% luck'. It is significant that luck plays so small a part. This factor alone links it more closely to chess and billiards than to any other games.

LEAVES

If you become good at maintaining a break it will be possible for you to get your first ball right round all the hoops in both directions and through the final, 'rover' hoop, all in one turn. Your ball then becomes a 'rover' and there is no more hoop for it to run – it has only to be pegged out. Do not do this yet, however, because you will need the ball as a helper ball to take your second ball round. A pegged out ball is out of the game, and normally it is a disadvantage to be one ball down to your opponent's two. If you have got round to the peg, though, you have now got to end your turn, because you will want to change balls; but you will want to leave the balls at the end of your turn to your opponent's least advantage. If possible, you will want to leave him with very little to do – the croquet equivalent of 'snookered'.

There is a variety of so-called 'leaves', and the one you need to aim for is the one which is bad for your opponent but good for you to pick up from. It isn't always possible to achieve both, and how you leave the balls will also depend on what state the game is in, and your assessment of your opponent's skill relative to your own. You may be able to leave your opponent's balls either side of a hoop or of the peg

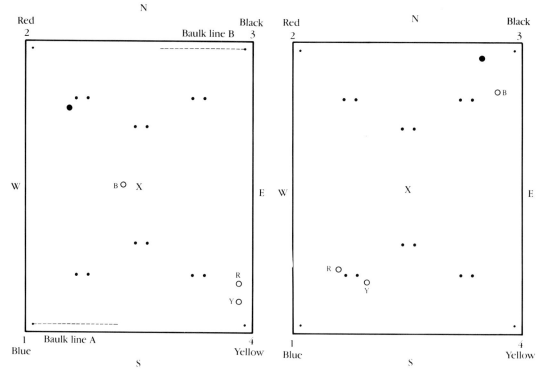

Fig. 11   A leave: Red and Yellow have to go on even if it's a case of their being allowed to 'lift' and play from either baulk-line.

Fig. 12   Leaving Red and Yellow 'wired'.

('crosswired' or 'crosspegged') so that he cannot shoot at one with the other. Since under the Laws if you do this you must leave him a ball to shoot at, you will leave one of your own a long way away so that your opponent will be forced to hit in, his chances of actually making a roquet being slight. If he fails, and you have kept your two balls together, one of his balls will now be near you and you will be able to use it to establish a three-ball break.

The golden rule for cross-wiring your opponent is to do so at your next hoop in order – where you can pick him up and use him. Crosswiring is less to delay him than to make things easier for you.

PEGGING OUT

Let's be optimistic and assume that you get the innings back, and brilliantly get your second ball all the way round to become a rover, too. Now you are ready to *peg out*. But you must still beware. Imagine that both your balls (say you're playing blue and black) are near the peg. Only a rover can peg out another rover, so you've no problem there. You make a roquet on black with blue, but you hit it too hard, and black is rushed onto the peg! Why does your opponent smile thinly? Why do you tear your hair? Because after making a roquet *you must take croquet*, but you have pegged black out on the roquet stroke and it is out of the game. You have nothing, therefore, to take croquet from. You lose your turn. Now you are not only at a disadvantage, but positively at your opponent's mercy. Only serious mistakes on his part will enable you to peg out your remaining ball and win the game.

The sequence for pegging out is: roquet (gently if necessary), then: croquet – to – peg out; then you peg out your striker's ball with the continuation stroke. A miss at this stage brings the whole house of cards down, so be careful. Croquet puts the nerves through hell!

PRACTICE

When you are not playing, try to get as much practice as you can – and pay special attention to hoop-running and to getting round on breaks. Practise picking up breaks, too – a job which is much more difficult to do than playing one, because you have to hang on to the innings while you're doing it – if you don't, your opponent takes over and either undoes, or worse, profits from, all your hard work.

Practise strokes – you'll probably feel that the stop-shot is the easiest to play, and the pass-roll the most difficult, though oddly enough I found the opposite to be true. Experiment with split-shots. Some people will advise you that one way of playing safe is to use as many stop-shots as possible and as few rolls and take-offs, but my advice is to be prepared for anything.

Watch other players, and analyse what they are up to. However, a word of caution here. Beginners watching advanced players will probably not understand what on earth they are doing. This is because they are up to bits of arcane strategy useful in advanced play but only confusing and misleading until you graduate to a level in the game where they can be applied. The vast majority of players will never reach, or want to reach, such heights, and the number of people who do so is relatively small.

As you practise and improve, you will find increasingly that things come naturally. Once you've grasped the basic techniques, you'll find that at the beginning of a season you won't need too long to get your eye in again – in this respect, croquet's like riding a bicycle or swimming: once learnt, never forgotten.

Don't be afraid to experiment and take chances either. If you don't, you'll never advance. At worst, if you are too conservative, you run the risk of becoming an 'Aunt Emma' player. These people are the bane of croquet courts, with their timid but viperish technique of keeping their own balls together, but taking off to split up the opponent's balls, then returning to home base to crawl towards a hoop, which they will only run if it is utterly safe, when the whole boring process is repeated. The average game of croquet might last two and a half to three and a half hours. Aunt Emma can stretch it out far longer, and in any case makes one hour seem like three. It is not even as if his style of play carries any particular advantage, because if he comes up against even a passably good regular player, who can create breaks, he can be outmanoeuvred and vanquished.

16 HANDICAPS AND PEELING

HANDICAPS

Croquet players who play at club and tournament level are given a handicap to play off. The CA is encouraging as much inter-club play as possible to make sure that individual clubs do not become isolated and develop handicaps at variance with the national norms. There is a Handicap Co-ordination Committee, whose job is to 'police' handicapping nationally. Handicapping is a system of assessment based on a scale of sixteen to minus five. An unknown 'outsider' joining a club, unless he is a self-confessed beginner, will be given a handicap of around nine until he has played enough to be graded up or down to his correct standard. It will take most beginners a season to get settled into the game, and then, if they have any talent for it, they will move up the scale fairly rapidly over the next two seasons or so.

Broadly speaking, the classes of player are divided by handicap in the following way:

A Class: one or less
B Class: one to five
C Class: six to ten
D Class: eleven to sixteen

The really top-flight players' handicaps will be around minus two.

Croquet also operates a bisque system in relation to handicaps. Note that this system does not apply to Advanced Play.

A 'bisque', says Law 38, 'is an extra *turn* given in handicap play'.

It is, if you like, a free go, and you can score points with it, though you must play it with the ball you used in your preceding turn. There also exists a half-bisque, which is a free go with which points cannot be scored. As things are at present constituted, the number of bisques you get is determined by the difference between your handicap and your opponent's. Say you have a handicap of ten, and your opponent has a handicap of six and a half. You get three and a half bisques. However, many croquet players today feel that there would be great advantages to be gained from the introduction of a *full-bisque game* (that is to say, in the example given above, you would get ten bisques and your opponent would get six and a half). This system in a modified form already exists in short croquet, and there is little doubt that it will come to the full-size game soon.

The great thing about a bisque is that you can take one at any time, and you can take one after another. The only thing you can't do is convert a full bisque into two half-bisques. For any player who is still improving his game a bisque is a godsend if he has botched a shot, for it gives him a chance to redeem his error. If you are playing a much better opponent, and therefore have a lot of bisques, do not be sparing of them but use them generously to get yourself off to a good start. If you do not, and your opponent gets the innings, you may find yourself being beaten despite the fact that you still have a number of bisques in hand. Players defeated in this unfortunate position are said to 'go to bed with their bisques' – and very silly it can make you feel!

PEELING

A peel is achieved when the striker's ball causes the object ball to run its hoop in order; the object ball may be the striker's partner ball, or an opponent ball – for on occasion it can be strategically of benefit to peel your opponent through, and even to peg him out to leave him one ball down. An Irish peel is achieved when both striker's and object ball go through the hoop they are both 'for' together. The word 'peel' derives from its inventor, Walter Peel.

What I have just described is a single peel, and although not necessarily common, they are not necessarily rare either. But there are other, multiple peels too: double, triple, quadruple, quintuple, and sextuple. I am only briefly going to describe the standard triple and the sextuple. Firstly, it will be interesting to see why they were developed at all.

In a game between good players, where there was little likelihood of anyone breaking down, it became increasingly likely that the player who got in first would take his first ball right round to the peg, leave the balls in an impossible situation for his opponent to do anything with, and then get in again with his second ball, go right round to the peg with it, peg both balls out – and win. At advanced level, games began to get very one-sided and rather tedious. Something had to be done. Various emendations to the rules were introduced, and finally a significant variation in the Laws, to be applied in Advanced Play, was introduced to upset this smooth progress to the peg. Basically, the new Law provides that 'if the striker's ball scored 1-back *or* 4-back for itself in the preceding turn', the opponent has the option of lifting either of his balls and playing it back into the game from either baulk line. The Law further provides that 'if the striker's ball scored 1-back *and* 4-back for itself in the preceding turn and its partner ball had *not* scored 1-back *before* that turn' the opponent may not only start his turn with the lift option described, but if he chooses he may instead put either of his balls *in contact* with any other ball and take croquet forthwith.

The triple peel was already in existence, but was now developed into a tactical manoeuvre (the Whichelo variation, introduced in 1946) to counter this new law. It works like this: you are playing, let's say, blue and black. Blue hasn't made a hoop yet but you've taken black straight around to 4-back. there you stop, because if you go through 4-back with it you'll have to concede the contact described above. As it is, since you've made 1-back in the turn, you have to concede the lift, but again you leave the balls in such a way as to give your opponent the least advantage. If he fails to get the innings, you then start taking your blue ball round. On the way, you peel black through 4-back when blue is for 3, through penultimate when blue is for 6, and through rover when blue is also for rover (or, if you can, when blue is going to 2-back or 3-back). You do not have to stop and concede anything because although your blue striker's ball has scored 1-back and 4-back in the turn, your black partner ball *has* scored 1-back before that turn. Provided you don't break down, you are home free.

The sextuple peel is similar, except that this time you stop your first turn before black runs 1-back. Both Keith Wylie and John Solomon have developed leaves at this position to thwart your opponent, but everything really has to be *exactly* positioned if the strategy is to work. Let's say your opponent fails to get the innings. You now switch to blue but you are confronted with the task of peeling black through all

64 Stephen Mulliner starting a successful triple peel on his opponent's ball. Roehampton, 1985. (*P L Alvey*)

six last hoops as you go round with blue. Of course, this means that you do not even have to concede a lift to your opponent, but the job you have set yourself is a monumental challenge.

Do not despair if the sextuple peel sounds beyond you: John Solomon himself only completed it once in his career. Keith Wylie achieved the first ever *delayed* sextuple leave – which he now prefers to call a '1-back leave' – and went on to carry it through in 1970. John Prince of New Zealand has also achieved a standard sextuple, and it may be that others have too, but you could count them on the fingers of one hand.

Triple peels are a little more common, and certinly something to aspire to, but don't be too disheartened if you don't make it. They don't occur that frequently even during the President's Cup, and they remain in the realm of the top two dozen players only. So be careful when you try to impress with talk of them! Their concept, however, is so beautiful that it seems a great shame that all players shouldn't at least be allowed to have a crack at them. One word of caution, however – a player with a greater handicap than 2 or 3 may find the frequency with which he fails to bring off a 'triple' dispiriting. There is, however, an alternative ploy to stopping before 4-back in anticipation of a triple

peel. This is to take your ball right round to the peg and then concede
a contact, but leave the balls so that it's impossible for your opponent
to do anything constructive with them. This is called a contact leave
and may involve leaving all the balls on the boundary, separated by
10–20 yards. Your opponent can take contact from any one of these,
but he will be hard put to it to even make one hoop. The contact leave
is not, however, the easiest thing in the world to pull off, either.

17 VARIATIONS ON A THEME

In this chapter I give you some of the many variations of croquet that can be played with the same equipment. There is nothing to prevent you playing the American 'nine wicket' game with regular croquet mallets and hoops, but you will need three extra hoops and an extra peg to do so.

A SHORTER GAME

The simplest variations are those which shorten the real game, but which must not be confused with 'short' croquet. The Laws provide that you may play a 22-point game, in which you simply use hoop 3 as the starting hoop, or an 18-point game. In this, you can either start on hoop 5, or start on hoop 1 but take the peg as next in order after hoop 2-back; or you can modify the setting by removing the two centre hoops – in which case you go straight to 1-back after running 4, and the peg is next in order after 4-back; or you start on hoop 1, but as soon as one of the balls of a side runs or is peeled through hoop 1 in order, hoop 3-back becomes the next point in order for that ball's partner ball, and the appropriate clip is placed on 3-back immediately. This last variation is for singles play only.

You can also play a 14-point game in which you simply cut out the 'back' hoops, and the peg is next after hoop 6.

TIME LIMITS

Time limits are sometimes imposed on tournament games. A tournament manager is allowed to set one of not less than three hours (two and a half in a weekend tournament). Once the time-limit has been reached play continues for an extension period for the striker to complete his turn and his opponent to play one following turn. If at the end of this period no-one is ahead, and thus the winner, play continues until the deciding next point is scored.

In America a time-limit of one and a half hours is imposed. At the end of that time the game simply ends; whoever is ahead winning. Under USCA Rules a time limit for each stroke is enjoined:

> A player should play his strokes as quickly as possible, and in doubles should avoid wasting time in prolonged discussion with his partner. (More than 75 seconds is considered excessive).

In US tournaments, each player is subjected to a forty-five second maximum for a shot, and in doubles each side is permitted two time-outs of forty-five seconds each. Time violations result in the loss of a turn, so it is pretty fierce. We'll return to differences between the USCA game and the 'International' game later in this chapter.

Time limits, incidentally, can affect the tactics by which one plays, and the tactics employed might otherwise be considered suicidal. Say that two teams are playing in doubles and that they are more-or-less level. If it's team A's turn to play they might then well play their forward ball to the peg and peg it out – thus winning the game within the time limit, if properly judged. (Remember, a rover ball *can* peg itself out – provided it hasn't just made a roquet – or it can peg out another rover.) Such a tactic, of putting yourself one ball down when your opponent is hot on your heels, would be ill-advised in an open-time game. On the whole, timed games do not seem to be a good idea, and are only to be used *faute de mieux*. A limited-hoop game is better.

DOUBLE GAMES

Croquet can be played as a doubles or a singles game. In doubles, each player has one ball, and in handicap doubles, a more experienced player is paired with a less experienced one. Strategy is affected in handicap doubles, for the better player generally has to think for both people, and set up the balls in his turn favourably for his partner's turn. The either-ball game is still played, but it may not always make sense for the better player to take his ball right round to the peg before 'coming back' to 'help' his partner round. The temperament and the psychological make-up of the weaker partner will affect the tactical thinking of his stronger 'shepherd'.

DOUBLE-BANKING

In tournaments where few courts are available, a game may be double-banked rather than time-limited. This involves two games being played on the same court simultaneously, a set of second-colour balls being introduced to avoid confusion. This is not done in the USA. The balls are colour-related thus:

blue – green
red – pink
black – brown
yellow – white

Strict rules of court etiquette apply in a double-banked game. People playing just for fun might like to invest in a set of second-colour balls, four more mallets, four more hoops, another peg and a book of Victorian rules and play the games as their ancestors played it! Beware, though, that such games can be very long, with long periods of inactivity for the outplayers. All the extra equipment would tot up to a fair sum, and you would need second-colour clips too!

WINTER CROQUET

Other variations of the game are almost legion: provided everybody plays to the same rules, there is no reason why people playing for fun shouldn't introduce them. Veronica Carlisle told me about a very sympathetic 'winter variation' in which the striker was only allowed to run a maximum of three hoops in a turn so that the outplayer didn't get too cold waiting around.

MAKING THE GAME EASIER OR MORE DIFFICULT

One of the contradictions of the game is that adepts find it too easy, whilst neophytes find it too hard. In fact, though, it is possible to introduce simple variations to make the game easier or harder, as the taste of the players dictates. To make it harder, Bernard Neal suggests, it's a simple matter to reduce the width of the yard-line area to, say, 9 inches, which would make defence easier and attack harder; and conversely, to make it easier, to widen the yard-line area to 4 or even 5 feet. Any ball that has gone off the court must be replaced on the yard-line, remember, as well as any ball in the yard-line area after each stroke.

Another method of making the game more difficult for advanced players who felt the need of even greater challenges is this: the 'lift or contact' Law mentioned in chapter sixteen (page 155) in connection with triple peels and so on could be tightened up, so that instead of 1-back *or* 4-back/1-back *and* 4-back, before having to concede, restrict progress to 3-back, so that you'd need to bring off a quadruple-peel to finish. This would increase the difficulty of going out in two breaks to a near-impossible level!

SHORT CROQUET

Short croquet, the brainchild of Lionel Wharrad, who has perhaps done more than anyone else in recent years to bring croquet in from the cold, is one of the most exciting variations on the theme and the most recent. You could call it croquet-for-our-time, since it requires less time and space than true croquet, but retains most of the real game's complexity. Short croquet brings the game into more people's reach, for many gardens could accommodate its 16 yard × 24 yard court. In fact, provided the 3 : 2 proportions are retained, there's no reason why the court shouldn't be smaller still. At club level, two tennis courts could double as three short croquet courts. Because of taking up less time and space, short croquet is more intensive, and the people-to-space/time ratio is dramatically reduced.

Great hopes, too, are had for short croquet's future as a television spectator sport, though many players have reservations about this, principally because its laws and its strategy are very close to the true game, and may not be simple enough to be grasped visually. Even with expert commentary (and those who have tried it testify how demanding the delivery of croquet commentary can be), informed television production and editing, and the fact that the court has been designed deliberately to fall within the scope of a single-angle camera shot – compare the Wimbledon lawn tennis general view of Centre Court – it may be some time before croquet is truly 'sold' as a television sport. the CAs on both sides of the Atlantic remain convinced, however; and indeed if such visually unpromising games as bridge and darts can enjoy a following on television, why not croquet, which is more interesting to watch; and just as arresting as snooker – *provided you know what is going on.*

Short croquet is laid out exactly like the full-size game, but the red-crowned hoop is the 6th, because the course is only run once. With certain modifications, a full-bisque game is played, and better players are required to complete a minimum number of peels to make play more equal. Because the court is so much smaller, older or frailer players are not disadvantaged by being too weak to bring off long shots – there are none to speak of.

The object of the game is to get both your balls through the six hoops and pegged out before your opponent. Toss a coin to decide who goes first. The first four turns are played to get the four balls on to the court, from either baulk line (or start line, as it is called in short croquet).

Play is then continued exactly as in croquet, using the roquet, croquet and continuation strokes, running the hoops in order, and so on. The yard lines are the same as for a full-size court, as are the proportions of all the court equipment.

GOLF CROQUET

Golf croquet, usually played on a full-size court, *can* be played on any size court. It does have a serious following, and its own tournaments, but most croquet players will feel the need of something meatier after a time. Golf croquet might be a contender for a televised spectator sport, but it does not serve as an introduction to the real game, for it has very little to do with it. It is in fact totally misnamed, for it has little to do with golf, and the croquet stroke is not used! The similarity with golf is that everyone is going for the same hoop at the same time, but unlike golf the balls are allowed to interfere with each other.

The balls are paired black-blue, yellow-red, and doubles or singles may be played. A short game consists of running the six croquet hoops forward and back, followed by hoop 3 again as decider (13 points). A long game (19 points) involves running the hoops forward and back, and then 1-back to rover again, with hoop 3 as decider again. The rules are as follows:

1 All balls are always for the same hoop and a point is scored for the side whose ball first runs the hoop in order. Everybody then moves on to the next hoop.
2 Each turn consists of one stroke only. There is no croquet stroke, no continuation stroke, and so on.
3 The balls are played in sequence: blue, red, black, yellow, blue, red etc.
4 The side that wins the toss can choose whether or not to lead, or the colour balls to play. The other side gets the choice not taken.
5 The balls are played into the game during the first four turns from baulk line B, only.
6 The score is kept as in golf; the game is won when one side is more points up than the number of points which remain available to be scored.
7 The jump-shot is not allowed.
8 The setting is as for croquet and the hoops are run in the same way. The peg, although set, plays no part in the proceedings.

Golf croquet is a useful introduction to croquet in so far as it teaches hoop running, and correct placing of your ball – thus encouraging you to get your eye in. It is also a more sociable game, because unless you are taking it very seriously it requires less concentration. As each turn consists of only one stroke, it is a much faster game, and if you wanted to ring a change on it you could easily introduce four more mallets and a set of second-colour balls and play as four teams of two, or two teams of four, or eight individuals, and have a regular party out there.

USCA RULES

It's possible that you may find yourself playing in the United States, or in Bermuda, Costa Rica, Jamaica or Mexico – all of which play by USCA Rules, so it's worthwhile to be aware of the principal differences, some of which we've touched on already. In the United States there are now clubs in every single state except, at the time of writing, Utah and Idaho, so you should pack your mallet if you're going over there!

In general, where there is a difference, the Americans have stuck to or revived an older rule.

The American game may be faster – but some would argue that their time limits alone are responsible for that. The American concept of 'deadness' (see below) may be seen as a counter-measure to Aunt Emma play, but one visiting English player writing in *Croquet* seemed to think there were more Aunt Emmas in the USA than there are in Great Britain, and most agree that 'deadness' deters break-building, which is a pity. There is something to be said on both sides, and British players who have played frequently in the USA, like Nigel Aspinall and Bernard Neal, have a professional respect for the American game. At the same time it seems sad that any rule differences should have grown up, especially in view of proposals for a World Croquet Federation.

The essential differences are these:

1 The 'yard line area' is 9 inches wide in the USA.
2 The game is started from a 'starting tee' one mallet's length from the front of hoop 1 and each ball is 'dead' (ie may not roquet or croquet) until that hoop has been run.
3 The balls are played in sequence. The International 'either ball' rule does not obtain.
4 Roqueting off-court results in your turn ending (this cramps International style, where deliberate roqueting off court is sometimes advantageous – for example, in one approach to the four-ball break).
5 Rover hoop is run *in the same direction* as hoop 5.
6 The concept of 'deadness'. We have seen that under the International Laws, you can roquet and then take croquet off each other ball. You then have to run your hoop in order if you want to repeat the exercise in the same turn, but if you fail to, and your turn ends, you can commence roqueting and croqueting regardless at the beginning of your next turn. Under USCA rules, however, you cannot do this: however many turns it takes, you must run your hoop in order before you are once more allowed to roquet and croquet the other balls. In other words, you carry your last turn's 'history' with you to the next: your slate is not wiped clean. You are said to be 'dead' on a ball which you may no longer roquet or croquet. The Americans have devised a 'deadness board' which is essentially a colour-coded scoreboard which acts as an *aide-memoire* on who is 'dead' on what.

In addition to these principal differences in the laws, there are one or two minor differences in terminology: in America, a peg is called a stake, and hoops are called wickets (they are fond of referring rather archly to their 'wicket ways').

AMERICAN 'BACKYARD' CROQUET

There is another game played in America on a wider scale still. It is known as 'backyard' croquet, and it is played with wide wire hoops and small, lightweight rubber-ended mallets with small, light, plastic balls. It can be played with this equipment on practically any shape, size or quality of lawn. An upmarket version uses standard croquet equipment. The setting is reminiscent of a Victorian one, and has nine 'wickets' and two 'stakes'. One stake, near the centre of the Northern boundary, is the turning stake. The other, opposite it, is for starting and finishing.

As usual, singles or doubles can be played, and red and yellow play blue and black. The unofficial game has many forms, and many local variants, in most of which the croquet stroke is unknown. The rules outlined here are those laid down by USCA for backyard croquet:

The standard court is a rectangle, 50 feet × 100 feet, or smaller in the same 1:2 proportion, but smaller than 30 feet × 60 feet is not recommended by USCA.

The stakes are set midway along and 6 feet in from the North and South boundaries. The 1st and 7th wickets are 6 feet in from the stakes, and the 2nd and 6th wickets are 12 feet in from them. The 4th wicket is central, and the four outer wickets are 34 feet in from the North and South boundaries, and 6 feet in from the East and West boundaries, as shown in the diagram overleaf.

The object of the game is the same as that of croquet, except that there is a total of 28 wicket points and 4 stake points to be scored for each side.

A ball advances by running its wickets in order. But a ball which has made a roquet cannot in the same stroke cannon off the roqueted ball and score a point for itself.

The game is played in colour sequence. The sequence of strokes is as for croquet but the concept of 'deadness' also applies. Hitting the upper

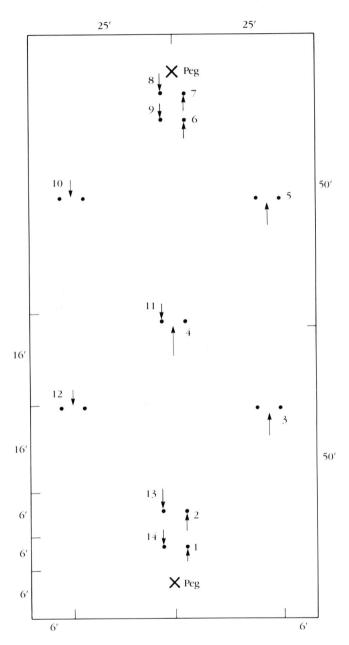

Fig. 13   American 'Backyard' croquet.

(or turning) stake entitles you to a continuation stroke, and may also clear 'deadness'.

Continuation strokes are not cumulative.

You start from a tee-off point three feet in front of wicket 1, and once struck, the ball is 'alive' on all the other balls (unlike USCA regular croquet, where the first wicket must first be run).

Only rover balls may peg themselves out or peg other rovers out.

Should an opponent cause a rover ball to hit the final stake, the player of that rover ball must take two turns out, and on the third place his ball one mallet length from the final stake but hit towards the upper stake. He must hit the upper stake before returning to the final stake as a 'reconstituted' rover. While engaged in trying to hit the upper stake, no matter how many turns he takes, no-one can play off him and he can play off no-one.

The game is otherwise governed by the Rules of USCA croquet although there are some special rules governing advanced play. Full details may be obtained from USCA (address in Appendix B).

INDOOR CROQUET

Indoor croquet is nothing new. An 1870 book of rules describes 'The Ladies' Game of Parlour Croquét':

> This game is one which is used in the long winter evenings, when darkness or the inclemency of the weather renders the outdoor game impossible. It is played in exactly the same way as the other, but in miniature; the amusement and excitement of Croquing is amply compensated for, by many pleasing incidents which occur in the more restricted area allowed by the size of the drawing-room or parlour.

Although modern indoor croquet is not played in quite such restricted circumstances, as it utilises sports halls which cover up to a full-size court area, it has not enjoyed enormous success yet. The reasons are not far to seek. It is difficult to find an adequate synthetic playing surface; it is difficult to anchor hoops sufficiently firmly in or through it, and, as croquet is so prodigal in its people/space/time ratio, lighting and heating of an indoor area become very expensive. With the advent of short croquet, however, and as croquet increases in popularity, it is possible that indoor croquet in one form or another will develop. Its advantages are clear: people could play the game all the year round; evening coaching sessions could be conducted after dark, and being able to play in warm and protected surroundings would be a boon for many frail, elderly or disabled players.

The Laws of indoor croquet are the same as for croquet, but one supposes that it will in practice become a form of short croquet, for economic reasons, and to maximise the use of any space available.

TABLE CROQUET

Table croquet is no more, sadly, though occasionally attempts are made to revive it. Jaques used to make sets, but would not consider doing so again until the game itself enjoyed the same kind of popularity that it had in Edwardian times. At present it would simply not be commerically sensible to market table croquet, for although the cost of the materials would be slight, the cost of the labour to create the tiny mallets, hoops and balls would be high. Even if a manufacturer produced a cheap plastic set the demand for it would hardly justify its existence; and the large dining tables or (preferably) full-size billiard tables on which table croquet used to be played are now largely a thing of the past in private houses.

Table croquet is played according to the same Laws as croquet, and enjoyed a considerable vogue in Edwardian England. A complete set in good condition today is a collector's item.

PARLOUR GAMES

Apart from table croquet, the game has not lent itself to many parlour versions, though an extremely ingenious board game called 'Crokey' based on the principles of croquet, was put on the market by Tactical Games of Ely in the mid-1970s, and sold to the USA, Australia and New Zealand as well as Great Britain. Also, within the last two years, a computer game based on croquet for use on BBC micro computers has been created by Allen Parker. The game is available from the Croquet Association.

KINGBALL

As we have seen, the variations rung by the Victorians on croquet were virtually limitless. 'Kingball' was a game in which the croquet stroke was only allowed to a ball which had become a rover (a 'Kingball'). A Kingball could either play a croquet stroke or a continuation shot after roqueting, but not both. No ball other than another Kingball could score points off a Kingball. And no ball was truly in play until it had run its first hoop.

THREE-SIDED CROQUET

Three-sided croquet (Jacques still supply a 6-mallet-and-ball family set) has several variations. It is possible to apply adapted normal rules to a three-sided game, provided that you play all the balls in in the first six turns. One variant, given an ordinary four-ball set, is to have three single players playing in sequence, and to use the fourth ball as a passive 'helper' in breaks. The first player to peg out his ball is the winner.

'PIRATES'

This game can be played by up to eight people. You play in sequence, and the first person to score 19 points wins. You can run hoops in any order and that scores you a point and gives you an extra stroke. But you can't immediately re-run the same hoop backwards to get another point! When you roquet another ball, you get an extra stroke (not a croquet stroke) and you also get all the unit points in that ball's score transferred to yours: ie, if the roqueted ball has scored 4 points, you get all 4 – it's the same up to 9; but if it's scored 11, you only get his 1 unit point – he keeps the 10, and you get nothing if you hit a ball with 10 points – there are no unit points. As in croquet, if you've hit *all* the other balls in one turn, you must run a hoop before you can hit them again in the same turn – but of course *any* hoop will do. If you wish, you can vary the setting and number of hoops for this game.

'CROQUET CASTLES'

The last variation on the theme of croquet comes from Lewis Carroll, who was a keen player himself. 'Croquet Castles' is perfectly playable and actually rather demanding, though you will need ten balls and five mallets. As you read, don't forget that this was written in 1863; but it shouldn't be too difficult for two families or groups of friends each owning a croquet set to club together to buy a set of second-colour balls and a couple of extra balls to be differentiated in some way from the eight others:

'CROQUET CASTLES'
(For Five Players)
I

This Game requires the 10 arches, and 5 of the 8 balls used in the ordinary game, and, in addition to them, another set of 5 balls, (matching these in colour, but marked so as to be distinct from them), and 5 flags, also matching them. One set of balls is called 'soldiers'; the other, 'sentinels'. The arches and flags are set up as in a figure, making 5 'castles', and each player has a castle, a soldier, and a sentinel; the sentinel's 'post' is half-way between the 'gate' and the 'door' of the castle, and the soldier is placed, to begin the game, just within the gate.

(N.B. The distance from one gate to the next should be 6 or 8 yards, and from the gate of a castle to the door 4 yards; and the distance from the door to the flag should be equal to the width of the door.)

[Using modern equipment, I make this a foot or so.]

II

The soldiers are played in order, then the sentinels, in the same order, and so on. Each soldier has to 'invade' the other 4 castles, in order, (eg soldier No 3 has to invade castles Nos 4,5, 1,2) then to re-enter his own, and touch the flag; and whoever does this the first, wins. To 'invade' a castle, he must enter the gate, go through the door, then between the door and the flag, then out at the gate again; but he cannot enter a castle, unless either the sentinel of that castle, or his own sentinel, be out of its castle.

(N.B. No ball can enter or leave a castle, except by passing through the gate.)

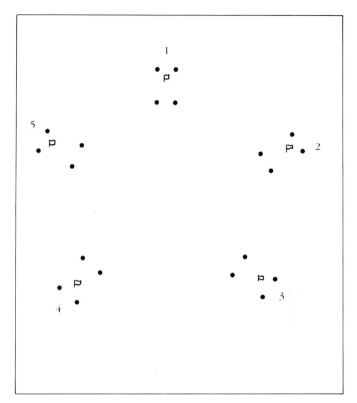

Fig. 14   Layout of court for 'Croquet Castles'.

III

If a sentinel touch a soldier, both being in the sentinel's castle, the soldier is 'prisoner'; he is replaced (if necessary) where he was when touched, the sentinel is placed in the gate, and the castle is 'fortified'. The prisoner cannot move, and nothing can go through the gate, till the castle is opened again, which is done either by the prisoner's comrade coming and touching the sentinel in the gate, or by the sentinel leaving the gate to go and rescue his own comrade; in the former case, both sentinels are replaced at their posts.

IV

When a prisoner is set free, he cannot again be taken prisoner until after his next turn.

V

If a ball touch another (except a prisoner, or a sentinel in his castle), the player may, if he likes, replace it where it was when touched, and use it to croquet his own with [a unique example of reverse tight croquet]: in the excepted cases, he must replace it, but can do no more.

VI

If a soldier go through an arch, or between a door and flag, in his proper course, or if a sentinel go through the gate of his castle, the player has another turn.

VII

A player, whose soldier is a prisoner, plays all his turns with his sentinel; and one, whose castle is fortified, with his soldier, unless it be taken prisoner, when he must play his sentinel to rescue it.

VIII

The sentinel of a fortified castle is considered to be in, or out of, the castle, as the owner chooses: that is, if he wishes to invade a castle, the sentinel of which is within it, he may consider his own sentinel as *out* of its castle (which gives him the right of invasion): or, if he wishes to go and rescue his soldier, he may consider it as *in* (so that he first plays it *through* the gate, and then has another turn).

CH. CH., OXFORD, May 4, 1863.

N.B. This game does not absolutely require more than *two* additional balls, beside those used in the ordinary game; these may be Light Blue and Light Green, and the 10 balls may be arranged as follows:

Soldiers	Sentinels
BLUE	LIGHT BLUE
BLACK	BROWN
ORANGE	YELLOW
GREEN	LIGHT GREEN
RED	PINK

Carroll does not mention how to determine order of play. I suggest lots or straws. Play is in sequence. The ball colours he mentions I would substitute thus:

BLUE	GREEN
RED	PINK
BLACK	BROWN
YELLOW	WHITE
NEW COLOUR 1	NEW COLOUR 2

18 THE LAST WORD

Finally, Walter Jones Whitmore's eight principles of play still seem so sound that I think they bear repeating:

1. Never pause too long on your stoke; the more especially if it is a difficult one. The mind winks as much as the eye; it is not capable of retaining an exact aim above a second or two at a time. You must not keep your attention too long on the stretch, but strike the moment you have it in your mind that you will hit, though without hurry.

2. In easy strokes, however, which merely require care, take plenty of time. If you count the occasions on which you get your balls wired from each other, or miss a hoop at the distance perhaps of two or three feet, you will find, nine times out of ten, that the accident was the result of mere carelessness.

3. Never allow yourself to consider too much the responsibility of a stroke. If the whole game depends on it you should yet play it as coolly, and with as little concern, as if it was the second stroke in the game.

4. *Nil desperandum*. The game is never lost till it is won. If you once consider your adversary as certain of the game, you have morally given up. After that every stroke you make is pretty certain to be timid, uncertain, and unsuccessful. Always, therefore, keep it in your mind that so long as you have another shot you have another chance. I have seen many a game pulled through by a steady hand, though both of the adversary's balls were 'pegging out'.

5 You must learn quickly, in every game, to estimate your adversary's powers correctly. If you can form an accurate idea at what distance he is tolerably sure, by what distance most puzzled, you can leave your ball at the end of each break so as to increase his difficulties as much as possible. Suppose he is very bad at long shots; directly you get your own balls together, keep his the whole length of the ground apart, and rather aim at this than at getting on rapidly with your own game. In course of time he falls into a chronic despair, loses all heart, and can do nothing with a break when he gets it. Therefore, play against the weakness of his character, as much as against the weakness of his game.

6 And whatever you do, never lose your temper. If you are fond of the game, and very fond of winning, and have yet schooled yourself to take every beating you get in a cheerful state of mind, you are likely very soon to be in the first flight amongst players. Apropos of this, pray, when you are unsuccessful, do not discover that you are playing with a wretched mallet, or that it is a ground which does not suit you, and is in favour of your adversary, or that it was too dark, or somebody was talking, &c. All these circumstances were as fair for one as the other. So 'take your spiritings' gently, and give all credit to the skill of the other side.

7 Against a good player win quick. The better the play, the fewer the breaks on both sides. When you have a skilful antagonist of good nerve against you, you must play a bold forward game, or not expect to win.

8 Don't think about your practice in the middle of a match. The same thing often occurs at croquet which happens so frequently at cricket. Many a player has gone out the first ball through being anxious about his attitude or action. He should have studied these in practice, not in play. All your energies should be simply given to getting the sight of the ball and to considering the means how best to defeat your adversary's plans.

APPENDICES

APPENDIX A

CROQUET EQUIPMENT

Buy the equipment you think you will need. Don't buy an expensive set if you're not going to use it much, or if you are unsure whether you will take to the game. On the other hand, I'd avoid sets which do not have full-size mallets and balls (unless you really only want something for the children to amuse themselves with, and I think children deserve better – don't forget that Solomon was handling a full-size mallet at the age of five).

I hesitate to mention prices, because they are out of date so quickly, but at the time of writing the top end of the market, a Jaques' 'Hurlingham' set, costs about £750 (and because of import duties, etc, $1600 in the USA). It's not necessary to spend nearly so much, but you should be prepared to part with around £250 if you want something nice.

The top-of-the-range sets provide you with corner flags, corner pegs, cast-iron hoops, a 'smasher', or small mallet for driving in the hoops, and even a 'Hoop drill' – an instrument for making holes to insert the hoops. None of these is really essential, and if later you want them, you can buy them separately. Top-range sets even come supplied with 'pegging-down pegs' sometimes called 'ball-marking pegs'. These look like outsize plastic drawing pins the colours of the balls and are used for marking the positions of the balls if a game is interrupted for any reason. They, too, can be bought separately. Lower down the scale, Jaques 'Standard' set costs about £140 at the time of writing, but I would go no lower than that.

I think you need a set containing the following minimum equipment: four hardwood mallets, four good quality plastic balls, six lightweight wrought iron hoops, a winning peg, and four clips. Buy a set for preference that comes in a wooden, not a fibre or cardboard, box. I see no special benefit in going for a box which is painted green or made out of mahogany, unless you really like it and can afford it. Jaques sells all equipment separately, so you could 'make up' a set if you wanted to, but they also offer a very wide range of sets. Incidentally, Jaques, who have been making sports equipment since 1795 – they started with billiard balls – cover a whole range of games as well as croquet. Their equipment sells worldwide. The Surrey head office will give you the address of their local agent.

Townsend Croquet Ltd was found in 1980 by Charles Townsend, a life-long croquet player, who is also a member of the Council of the Croquet Association and who has presented a trophy for the Junior Championship. Townsend's 'Championship' set will set you back a little over £300, but his more basic 'Grange' set at about £120 is pretty good. Townsend very roughly fills the gap in the market between Jacques' upper end and the very cheap 'Super Jouet' sets from France, which appear to offer value for money, but are not *true* croquet.

Walkers Croquet Equipment is the company which markets the mallets with plastic heads. That's putting it a bit crudely, because the hard-wearing white 'Duralon' head is guaranteed for five years and is very practical. Some people jib a little at a mallet like this, which has an aluminium shaft and a polyurethane grip, and looks very hi-tech, but for the more traditionally-minded Walker also produce a 'Permali' headed mallet. Walker makes mallets to individual specifications, and I think they represent good value for money in the middle range – about £40. Most of their mallet heads are square. Walker also market three sets – the 'Tournament', the 'Club' and the 'Basic'. I wonder if one day we might see sturdy, moulded plastic hoops?

Bernard Neal markets a no-nonsense mallet with an aluminium shaft, rubber handle and 'Permali' head. The mallet also comes in a deluxe version.

Ken Townsend, no relation to Charles Townsend, manufactures aluminium hoops and undertakes expert mallet repairs. For the latter service he usually has quite a long waiting-list.

If I were buying my first croquet set, I think I would plump for Jaques 'Challenge', or, if I had a little less money in my purse, for Townsend's 'Grange'. But don't take my advice: go and look at what's on offer, and send for brochures. The manufacturers will tell you where your local suppliers are. In London, Harrods and Lillywhites stock croquet equipment.

ADDRESSES:

John Jacques & Son Ltd
Whitehorse Road
Thornton Heath
Surrey CR4 8XP
Tel: 01 684 4242

Townsend Croquet Ltd
Claire Road
Kirby Cross
Frinton-on-Sea
Essex CO13 0LX
Tel: 025 56 4404

Walker Croquet Equipment
82 Queen's Crescent
Chippenham
Wiltshire SN14 0NP
Tel: 0249 654319

Bernard Neal
Moat Cottage
Kidnappers' Lane
Leckhampton
Cheltenham
Gloucestershire GL53 0NR
Tel: 0242 510624

Ken Townsend
Mispah
11 Knights Avenue
Tettenhall
Wolverhampton WV6 9QA
Tel: 0902 752975

Your local garden centre will be able to advise you on contractors who will undertake the laying of a croquet lawn. In the south-east, you might contact John Waterer, Sons & Crisp Ltd in Ascot. Their telephone number is 0990 28081.

APPENDIX B

CROQUET ABROAD

Croquet is played all over the world, but – outside Great Britain – principally in Australia, New Zealand and the USA. It *is* played in Europe – there are clubs in Portugal, Russia, Spain, Sweden and Switzerland. There are individual players or private clubs in Belgium, France (where it is terribly upper class) and Holland. There are a few players in Italy, but none at all that I can trace in Germany. Charles Townsend presented his croquet equipment at a Trade Fair in Munich and was met only with bewilderment: 'Cricket?' they ventured.

Here are the addresses of some clubs and associations which might be useful to you if you are a travelling player:

Australian Croquet Council
39 Fourth Avenue
South Perth
6151 W. Australia

Canadian Croquet Association
159 Walmer Road
Toronto M5R 2X8
Canada

CERN Croquet Club
CH-1211 Geneva
Switzerland

(CERN is the European Organisation for Nuclear research. The club has fifteen members, of whom three are Swiss.)

Helsingborg Croquet Society
Samuelsgatan 28, 252, 59
Helsingborg
Sweden

New Zealand Croquet Council
11 Kiwi Street
Alice Town
Lower Hutt
New Zealand

Santa Clara Club
Villacarla
Por-Vera 6
Jerez de la Frontera
Spain

South African Croquet Association
The Good Erf
6 Glen Avenue
Constantia
Cape Town 7800
South Africa

Tasmania Croquet Association
135 Derwent Avenue
Lindisfarne
Tasmania 7015
Australia

If you are interested in croquet in Japan, contact:

Professor Ikeda
University of Tsukuba
Institute of Health & Sports Sciences
Tsukuba Science City
Japan

APPENDIX C

PRINCIPAL CLUBS IN EIRE,

GREAT BRITAIN AND THE USA

With more public clubs, Sports Council aid, and the advent of the short version, croquet has become as accessible as any other game. The garden croquet player who wishes to take the game more seriously could do worse than join the CA – details of the reasonable fees, which permit free entry to tournaments, are available from the Administration Secretary, whose address is given in chapter ten (page 98). There is no need, however, to be a member of the CA to be a member of a club, though it is an advantage.

In the Republic of Ireland, contact:

Carrickmines Croquet & Lawn Tennis Club
Carrickmines
Co. Dublin
Eire

In Great Britain, the Croquet Association will give you the addresses of clubs in England. Here are some of the principal ones:

Bristol Croquet Club
Shirehampton Road
Stoke Bishop
Bristol

Edgbaston Croquet Club
Richmond Hill Road
Edgbaston
Birmingham

Bowdon Croquet Club
St Mary's Road
Bowdon
Cheshire

Budleigh Salterton Croquet Club
Westfield Close
Upper Stoneborough Lane
Budleigh Salterton
Devonshire

Cheltenham Croquet Club
Old Bath Road
Cheltenham
Gloucestershire

Roehampton Club
Roehampton Lane
London SW15

Southport Croquet Club
Victoria Park
Rotten Row
Southport
Merseyside

Hunstanton Croquet Club
Lynn Road
Hunstanton
Norfolk

Nottingham Croquet Club
Highfield
University Boulevard
Nottingham
Nottinghamshire

Southwick Croquet Club
Victoria Road
Southwick
Brighton
West Sussex

In Scotland, there are lots of clubs, including Gleneagles, Strathcona and the Trossachs. Contact the Scottish Croquet Association at:

17 Greygoran
Sanchie
Clackmannanshire FK10 3ET
Scotland
Tel: 0259 213515

In the USA, there are various sorts of clubs – family, private, country, hotel, university, and so on. One club, Birnam Wood, at Santa Barbara, California, plays 'International' rules. American Rules USCA croquet is played in Bermuda, Canada, Costa Rica, The Bahamas, Jamaica and Mexico. Principal clubs are located in Arizona, California, Florida, Illinois, New York and Rhode Island, but there are clubs in virtually every state. For addresses, contact:

United States Croquet Association
500 Avenue of the Champions
Palm Beach Gardens
Florida 33418
Tel: (305) 627 3999

Croquet International Ltd are agents for Jaques equipment in the States. Write to them c/o the USCA. Other main croquet equipment suppliers there are:

Forster Manufacturing Co Inc
Wilton
Maine 04294
USA

and Skowhegan Croquet, who make the Challenge sets, a good 9-wicket set in a canvas carrying-bag for a reasonable $200. Order from Croquet International at USCA.

APPENDIX D

PRINCIPAL UK TOURNAMENTS,

AND THE MACROBERTSON SHIELD

There are very many prizes to be competed for at over 100 events during the season (end of March – beginning of October), among which are:

The National Short Croquet Team Event
The British Universities Croquet Championships (Reeve Cup)
The Inter-Schools Team Championship (Rothwell Shield)

NATIONAL EVENTS

The Inter-Club Championship (Final in early October)
The Mary Rose Inter-Club Trophy (Final in early October)
The Longman Club Team Cup (Final in early October)
The Secretary's Shield
(Both The Mary Rose Inter-Club Trophy and The Secretary's Shield were presented by Richard Rothwell.)

CHAMPIONSHIPS

The British Open Championships (July)
     Croquet Championship
     Doubles Championship
     Association Plate
The British Men's & Women's Championships ('The Caskets') (June)
     Men's
     Women's

Mixed Doubles
Du Pre Cup
Ladies' Plate Event
The National Junior Championship (August)
      Junior (Charles Townsend Cup) Advanced Play
      Plate Event

INVITATION EVENTS

President's Cup: open to the best eight CA players by invitation from the CA Council (early September)
Chairman's Salver: for the second best eight (early September)
Spencer Ell Cup: for the third best eight (early September)
– these events are known as the 'Eights'.
      Selectors' weekend
      Ladies' Field (Barlow Bowl): best six CA women players.
      Longman Bowl: for the second best six women.

REPRESENTATIVE MATCHES

Home Internationals (end of May)
      UK/Wales/Scotland/Ireland
The MacRobertson Shield
This now takes place every four years and is hosted in sequence by Great Britain, New Zealand and Australia. The record shows British dominance of the event:

Year	Host	Winner
1925	England	England
1927	Australia	Australia won on games
1930	Australia	Australia
1935	Australia	Australia
1937	England	England
1950	New Zealand	New Zealand
1956	England	England
1963	New Zealand	England
1969	Australia	England
1974	Great Britain	Great Britain
1978	New Zealand	New Zealand
1982	Australia	Great Britain
1986	Great Britain	New Zealand

In the early years, the event was spasmodic, owing to funding problems, and not all three countries always participated. There was also a long gap caused by the Second World War. Since 1974 the whole of Great Britain has been represented by the six-person team.

APPENDIX E

BASIC LAWS OF ASSOCIATION CROQUET AND GOLF CROQUET

Reproduced by kind permission of B G Neal and the Croquet Association

These basic laws cover all that needs to be known by those who are learning to play and enjoy Association Croquet. However, complex situations occur from time to time which are not dealt with here. These are covered in the full Laws, to which reference is made in appropriate places. The full Laws, available from the Croquet Association, are the final and only authority and are accepted as such in countries where Association Croquet is played, notably Great Britain, Australia, New Zealand and South Africa.

COURT & SETTING (LAW 1)*

Standard Court

1   The standard court is a rectangle 35 yards by 28 yards (Fig. 1). The boundary is marked, usually with a continuous white line. One yard in from the boundary are the yard-lines, which are not marked. The area between the yard-lines and the boundary is termed the yard-line area.

2   The four corners are called corners 1, 2, 3 and 4. They may be marked with decorative flags (Fig. 2).

3   Corner pegs mark positions on the boundary one yard from the corner flag (Fig. 2). In each corner the yard-lines meet at the corner spot. Corner flags and corner pegs may be temporarily removed by the striker if they impede him.

4   13 yard lengths of the yard-line, from the corner spots at corners 1 and 3 towards corners 4 and 2 respectively, are called baulk-lines A and B (Fig. 1).

* References are made throughout to the Laws contained in LAWS OF ASSOCIATION CROQUET AND GOLF CROQUET (1984 edition).

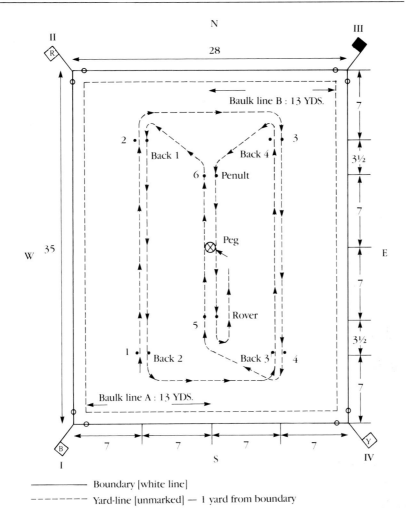

———————— Boundary [white line]

‑ ‑ ‑ ‑ ‑ ‑ ‑ ‑ Yard-line [unmarked] — 1 yard from boundary

Corners where yard-lines meet are called corner spots
Corner hoops [1,2,3,4] are 7 yards in from either side of boundary
Centre hoops [5,6] are 14 yards in from N.G.S boundaries and 10.5
yards in from E.G.U. boundaries
Starting hoop [1] has blue crown

Final hoop [Rover] has red crown
Arrows show direction of play [in US rules Rover is run in same
direction as 5]

5 There is a centre peg and six hoops whose setting is shown in Fig. 1. The order of making the hoops and the peg is indicated by the arrows.

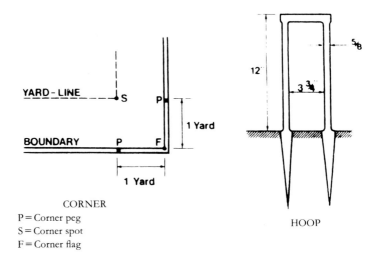

P = Corner peg
S = Corner spot
F = Corner flag

CORNER

HOOP

Modified Court

6 If the area available is too small for a standard court, a modified court may be used, maintaining the same ratios of the dimensions. The yard-line remains one yard in from the boundary.

EQUIPMENT & ACCESSORIES (LAWS 2 & 3)

7 *Hoops*
The hoops are made of metal and are painted white. Their dimensions are shown in Fig. 3*. The crown of the first hoop is coloured blue and of the last hoop (known as the rover) red. Each hoop must be firmly fixed in the ground.

8 *Centre Peg*
The centre peg is made of wood, $1\frac{1}{2}$ inches diameter and 18 inches high.

9 *Balls*
There are four balls, coloured blue, black, red and yellow. Each ball is $3\frac{5}{8}$ inches diameter and weighs approximately 1 lb.*. (Alternative coloured balls green, brown, pink and white are permitted.)

10 *Mallets*
The head of the mallet is usually made of wood and the two end faces must be identical.

* Lighter balls and hoops of different design are normally used in Garden Sets.

11   *Clips*
     A clip of the same colour as the ball is placed on the hoop or peg next in
     order for each ball. For the first six hoops the clip is placed on the crown,
     and for the last six on an upright.

LEVEL SINGLES

12   One player plays the blue and black, and the other the red and yellow
     balls (or green and brown versus a pink and white).
13   The winner is the player who makes both his balls score the 12 hoop
     points and the peg point in the sequence shown in Fig. 1, a total of 26
     points, before his opponent.
14   The players have alternate turns. Except at the start of the game (see para.
     20) a player may play either of his two balls in his turn. The ball he
     chooses at the start of his turn must be played throughout that turn,
     during which it is known as the striker's ball.

Outline of the game (LAW 4)

The basis of the game is given in paragraphs 15–18. These are amplified in
subsequent paragraphs, which also cover some of the special situations which
arise in play.
15   A player is initially entitled to one stroke in a turn, after which his turn
     ends unless in that stroke his striker's ball has scored a hoop point or hit
     another ball.
16   When a hoop point is scored the striker is entitled to play one continuation
     stroke.
17   When the striker's ball hits another ball, the striker is said to have made
     a roquet on that ball and he becomes entitled to two extra strokes. The
     first of these is known as the croquet stroke. This is made after picking
     up and placing the striker's ball in any position in contact with the
     roqueted ball, which in the croquet stroke is now known as the croqueted
     ball. The striker then plays the croquet stroke by striking his own ball.
     After the croquet stroke the striker plays a continuation stroke.
18   During a turn the striker may roquet and take croquet from each ball
     once. If he runs his hoop in order he becomes entitled to roquet and take
     croquet from each ball afresh. Thus by a series of strokes the striker may
     make one or more points in a break.

Start of the game (LAWS 5 and 6)

19   The winner of the toss can take the choice of lead (i.e. to play first or
     make his opponent play first) or the choice of balls (i.e. to play with the

blue and black or with the red and yellow). If he takes the choice of lead the opponent has the choice of balls, and vice versa.

20 The first player plays either of his balls from any point on baulk-line A or B. At the end of that turn his opponent does likewise. In the third and fourth turns the remaining two balls are similarly played into the game. From the fifth turn onwards the striker may play either of his two balls in his turn (para. 14).

21 In these first four turns roquets can be made and hoop points scored.

Roquet (LAW 16)

22 The striker makes a roquet when his striker's ball hits a ball which he is entitled to roquet (para. 18). The roquet is made even though the hit is not direct, and is the result of glancing off a hoop or the peg or a previously croqueted ball.

23 A roquet is not made if croquet has already been taken in that turn from the ball which is hit, and the striker has not subsequently run a hoop in order (para. 18).

24 The turn does not end if the roqueted ball goes off the court. It is replaced on the yard-line at the point nearest to where it went off (on the corner spot if it went off between a corner peg and corner flag, Fig. 2). The striker then takes croquet. (Situations in which the roqueted ball, when replaced, is in contact with another ball are dealt with in LAWS 12, 16 and 19.)

25 The turn does not end if the striker's ball goes off the court after making a roquet. It is picked up and placed for the croquet stroke.

26 If at the beginning of a turn the striker elects to play a ball in contact with another ball, he is deemed to have made a roquet and immediately takes croquet (LAW 16).

27 When a roquet is made, the striker takes croquet, unless his turn has ended because

(i) the stroke was a croquet stroke during which the roquet was made and the croqueted ball was sent off the court (para. 29); or

(ii) the roqueted ball was pegged out in the stroke and is therefore removed from the court (paras. 42, 43).

Croquet Stroke (LAWS 19 and 20)

28 In the croquet stroke the croqueted ball must be moved or shaken (para. 49).

29 The turn ends if in the croquet stroke the croqueted ball is sent off the court.

30   The turn ends if in the croquet stroke the striker's ball goes off the court, unless

   (i) it scores a hoop point for itself in that stroke (para. 40), or

   (ii) it makes a roquet, in which case the striker then takes croquet (para. 32 (ii)).

31   Any ball which goes off the court as a result of a croquet stroke is replaced on the yard-line at the point nearest to where it went off (LAW 12).

Continuation Stroke (LAW 21)

32   After the croquet stroke the striker plays a continuation stroke unless

   (i) his turn has ended under para. 29 or 30; or

   (ii) he has made a roquet, in which case he takes croquet.

33   Continuation strokes are not cumulative, so that

   (i) if a roquet is made in a croquet stroke, the striker immediately takes croquet and then plays one continuation stroke (para. 32 (ii)).

   (ii) if the striker runs his hoop in order and then makes a roquet in the same stroke, he immediately takes croquet and then plays one continuation stroke (para. 38 (i)).

   (iii) if the striker runs his hoop in order in a croquet stroke, he plays one continuation stroke.

   (LAW 4 (g)).

Hoop points (LAW 14)

34   A ball scores a hoop point by running its hoop in order in the right direction (Fig. 1), except that if a ball goes through its hoop after making a roquet it does not score the hoop point in that stroke.

   If, however, while running its hoop in order, but before completing the running, the striker's ball hits a ball that is clear of the hoop on the non-playing side and has finally run the hoop when it comes to rest, the hoop is scored and a roquet made (LAW 17).

35   The front of the hoop as a ball approaches to run it in order is the playing side and the other side is the non-playing side. A ball begins to run a hoop only when the front of the ball passes the non-playing side, and completes the running when the back of the ball passes the playing side (Fig. 4) and stays through (wear of the turf within the jaws of a hoop sometimes causes the ball to roll back).

36   A ball may complete the running of a hoop in two or more turns.

37   If the striker is taking croquet from a ball which lies partly within the jaws of the striker's hoop in order, the striker's ball may run the hoop in the croquet stroke provided that when placed for the croquet stroke his ball has not begun to run the hoop.

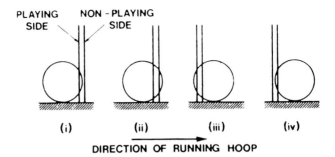

PLAYING SIDE · NON-PLAYING SIDE

(i)   (ii)   (iii)   (iv)

DIRECTION OF RUNNING HOOP

HOOP RUNNING

(i) Ball has not started to run the hoop
(ii) Ball has started to run the hoop
(iii) Ball has not completed running the hoop
(iv) Ball has completed running the hoop

38 When the striker's ball has scored a hoop point for itself he plays a continuation stroke, unless
    (i) he makes a roquet in the hoop stroke, in which case he take croquet, or
    (ii) his turn has ended by sending a croqueted ball off the court (para. 29).

39 When a ball other than the striker's ball is caused to run its hoop in order, it is said to have been peeled through the hoop and the hoop point is scored.

40 If the striker's ball goes off the court after running its hoop in order, the turn does not end. The ball is replaced on the yard-line at the point nearest to where it went off, and the striker plays his continuation stroke (LAW 12).

Peg point (LAW 15)

41 When a ball has scored all 12 hoop points it is known as a rover ball.

42 A peg point can only be scored when the striker's ball is a rover and
    (i) it hits the peg without first having made a roquet in that stroke, or
    (ii) it causes another rover ball to hit the peg (see para. 57 for handicap play).

43 A pegged-out ball is removed from the court at the end of the stroke.

Ball off the Court (LAW 10)

44 A ball goes off the court (regardless of where it finally comes to rest) as soon as any part of it would touch a straight edge raised vertically from the inside edge of the boundary.

At the end of each stroke all balls that go off the court, except the striker's ball when it has made a roquet (para. 25), are replaced on the nearest point on the yard-line.

Balls in the yard-line area (LAWS 11 and 12)

45 At the end of each stroke all balls in the yard-line area, except the striker's ball, are placed on the nearest point on the yard-line.

46 If the striker's ball is in the yard-line area it is played from where it lies unless the turn has ended, in which case it is also placed on the nearest point on the yard-line.

Wired balls (LAW 13)

47 A ball is wired from another ball if
    (i) a hoop or the peg would impede the direct course of any part of the striker's ball towards any part of the other ball, or
    (ii) the swing of the mallet prior to impact with the ball is impeded by a hoop or the peg, or
    (iii) any part of the striker's ball is within the jaws of a hoop.
    (See LAW 13 for precise definitions of wiring.)

48 If at the beginning of a turn the striker elects to play a ball
    (i) for whose position the opponent is responsible, and
    (ii) which is wired from all other balls, and
    (iii) which is not in contact with another ball,
he may lift that ball and play it from any position on baulk-line A or B. He may alternatively play it from where it lies.

Faults (LAW 32)

49 The striker commits a fault if when making a stroke he
    (i) pushes his ball
    (ii) hits his ball more than once (double tap)
    (iii) squeezes his ball against a hoop or the peg (crush)
    (iv) touches any ball with any part of his body or clothes
    (v) touches a ball other than his own ball with his mallet
    (vi) fails to move or shake the croqueted ball in a croquet stroke.
    (See LAW 32 for full definitions and descriptions of other faults; see also Customs of the Game, LAWS 44–51.)

50 When a fault has been committed the striker's turn ends, no point can be scored as a result of that stroke and the balls are replaced.

51 If the striker plays with a wrong ball, his turn ends and all the balls are replaced as they were before the mistake occurred (LAW 28). (See LAWS 26–35 and 38(h) for other errors and their penalties.)

MODIFIED GAME OF 14 POINTS (LAW 52)

52   This game is a shortened game in which each ball makes the first six hoop points and then the peg point.

HANDICAP GAMES

The foregoing Laws of Level Play apply with the following additions:

Bisques (LAW 38)

53   A bisque is an extra turn given in handicap play. A bisque turn can only be played by the striker with the ball with which he was playing in the previous turn. In a bisque turn the striker is entitled to make roquets and run hoops etc., exactly as in an ordinary turn.

54   A half-bisque is a turn in which no point can be scored for any ball. A bisque cannot be split into two half-bisques.

55   A player entitled to a bisque or a series of bisques may play one or more in succession at any time in the game when he is in play.

56   The number of bisques to be given is the difference between the handicaps of the two players.

57   A player may not peg out his own ball before his partner ball has become a rover, unless an opponent's ball has already been pegged out (LAW 39).

58   In a modified game (para. 52) the bisques given are scaled down in proportion to the number of points in the game (LAW 55).

DOUBLES (LAWS 40 and 43)

59   The game is played between two sides, each side consisting of two players. One player plays throughout with one ball of the side and his partner with the other.

60   In handicap doubles the number of bisques given is half the difference between the joint handicaps of the sides. In a full game a fraction of $\frac{1}{4}$ becomes a half-bisque and $\frac{3}{4}$ becomes a full bisque. (See LAW 55 for a shortened game.)

Either player of the side can take the bisques to which they are entitled.

SUMMARY

Some of the more important points are summarised below.

61   The balls are not played in the sequence blue, red, black, yellow. This is only done in Golf Croquet.

62   You can roquet and take croquet before you have scored a hoop.

63   When you run your hoop in order the slate is wiped clean and you may roquet and take croquet from each other ball again.

64   At the start of each new turn you are entitled to roquet and take croquet from each other ball, even though you may have roqueted them in previous turns.

65   If you have taken croquet from a ball, and before running your next hoop in order your striker's ball hits the same ball again, it is not a roquet and you cannot therefore take croquet.

66   You are entitled to a continuation stroke after playing a croquet stroke or running your hoop in order. But you are never entitled to two successive continuation strokes (para. 33).

67   You cannot put your foot on your ball in a croquet stroke (this is a fault and the turn ends).

68   Your *turn ends* if in any stroke except a croquet stroke you
     (i) do not make a roquet, or
     (ii) do not run your hoop in order.

69   Your *turn ends* if in a croquet stroke
     (i) the croqueted ball goes off
     (ii) your ball goes off, unless it makes a roquet or runs its hoop in order.

70   Your *turn ends* if you commit a fault in any stroke.

71   Your *turn ends* if you play a wrong ball.

72   Your *turn does not end* if you make a roquet and
     (i) the roqueted ball goes off
     (ii) your ball goes off.

73   Your *turn does not end* if you run your hoop in order and your ball then goes off.

74   If a rover ball is caused to hit the peg, it is not pegged out unless the striker's ball is a rover.

GOLF CROQUET

75   Singles or doubles can be played; the sides are blue and black against red and yellow.

76   The sides play alternately, and each turn consists of one stroke only. The laws of Association Croquet relating to roquet, croquet, continuation strokes and wiring do not apply.

77   The balls are played in the sequence blue, red, black and yellow. Therefore, if yellow is played on the first stroke, blue follows, then red and so on.

78   All balls are always for the same hoop in order. The point is scored for the side whose ball first runs the hoop.

79   In a 13-point game the first 12 hoops are as in Association Croquet (Fig. 1), and the last hoop is hoop 3. In a 19-point game the hoops 1-back to rover are repeated after rover is first made, and the last hoop is again hoop 3. The peg remains in its place but is not used as a point.

80   The side that wins the toss can either take the choice of lead, in which case the other side has the choice of balls, or the choice of balls, in which case the other side has the choice of lead.

81   In the first four turns the balls are played from any point on baulk-line B.

82   The score is kept as in golf, and the game is won when one side is more points up than the number of hoops remaining (e.g. 3 up and 2 to play).

83   To score a point the striker's ball or his partner ball must run the hoop completely (Fig. 4) as a result of the stroke, unless it had previously begun to run the hoop as a result of an opponent's stroke.

84   The striker must not send his ball to the next hoop instead of continuing to contest the hoop in order.

85   The striker must not attempt to make his ball rise from the ground (jump shot).

(See LAWS OF GOLF CROQUET 5 for errors
and 6 for handicapping.)

GLOSSARY

A-class player: one whose handicap is so low that he plays under Advanced Play Laws

all-round break: using one turn to get a ball round all the hoops, or, in Advanced Play, as far as 4-back

'Aunt Emma': a dull player, who fights shy of setting up breaks, and who makes hoops off his partner ball, but very slowly, using whole turns just to keep his balls together and his opponent's split up

ball in hand: a ball that must be picked up and placed elsewhere on the court; for example, on the yard line, or to take croquet

baulk line: starting line on North and South boundaries

bisque: a handicap game extra *turn*. You can score points with it, but you can't do so with a *half-bisque*

break: an unbroken sequence of strokes, involving two or more balls, by which the striker's ball runs a number of its hoops in order

break down, to: make an unsuccessful shot or commit a fault, thus causing your turn to end

corner, to: a defensive stroke playing a ball into a corner

Croquet Association, the: the governing body of the game in England

croquet stroke: in which the striker's ball is placed touching the roqueted ball, and hit, causing both balls to move

crosswire, to: to position two balls so that a hoop lies directly between them (*cross-pegging* is a similar tactic)

crown: top of hoop

crush: in which a ball is in contact with mallet and hoop or peg at the same time. Unless the stroke is being played *away* from the hoop or peg, this is a fault

cut rush: a rush played to send the object ball off at an angle to the direction of the stroke

double-tap: a fault in which the mallet hits the striker's ball twice in one stroke

fault: a foul

'for' a hoop, to be: to be aiming for that hoop next in order

hit, to: successfully make a roquet

hit in, to: make a long shot

hoop-bound: hampered in making a stroke by too-close proximity to a hoop

jaws: opening of hoop

'jawsed': when a ball is stuck in a hoop

leave: how the balls are *deliberately* left at the end of a turn

long (or 'high') bisquer: a player with a numerically high handicap

low (or 'short') bisquer: a player with a numerically low handicap

object ball: the target ball

one-ball shot: in which only one ball's direction is important

open shot: in which the striker's ball is able to hit any part of the object ball

outplayer: the one who doesn't have the innings

peel, to: cause the object ball, or the croqueted ball, to run its hoop in order

peg down, to: interrupt a game and mark the position of the balls with colour-coordinated pegging-down pegs

peg out, to: remove a ball from the game when it is a rover by causing it to hit the peg. Only a rover may peg itself or another rover out

pegged-out game: in which one or two balls are pegged out

penultimate (or 'penult'): the last hoop but one

push: a fault in which the mallet stays in contact with the ball too long after impact

roquet: in which the striker's ball hits another ball *from which it may then take croquet.* See Law 16

rover: the last hoop, which has a red crown

rover-ball: one which has run the rover hoop in order

run, to: successfully pass through a hoop in order

rush: a roquet that sends the roqueted ball to a predetermined position

scratch player: one whose handicap is zero

split shot: croquet stroke in which the balls move off in different directions

stake: US terminology for 'peg'

stalking: lining up a ball for a shot by approaching it purposely from a distance

tice: a shot which places a ball in a position designed to entice the opponent to shoot at it

wicket: US terminology for 'hoop'

wire: uprights of a hoop

wire, to: position balls so that they are crosswired from each other, or from their objective

yard line: unmarked line one yard in from the boundary, usually measured by a mallet's length

yard line area: the space between the yard line and the boundary; balls which end up here after a stroke are replaced on the yard line at the conclusion of the stroke.

BIBLIOGRAPHY

Cotter, E P C, *Tackle Croquet This Way* (Stanley Paul, 1960)

Crowther-Smith, H F, *A Croquet Alphabet* (Henry Stone, 1912)

——, *A Croquet Nonsense Book* (privately published, 1929)

——, *The Art of Croquet* (H F & G Witherby, 1932)

Elvey, George Frederick Handel, *Croquet: A Guide to the Strokes of the Game* (E J Larby, 1910)

Field, The, Croquet: its Implements and Laws, drawn up by a Committee of Players appointed by the Editor of The Field (Horace Cox, 1866)

General Conference of Croquet Clubs, *The Laws of Croquet adapted at the General Conference of Croquet Clubs on Jan. 19, 1870* (De la Rue, 1870)

Heath, James Dunbar, *The Complete Croquet Player* (Routledge, 1874)

Jaques, John, *Croquet, the Laws and Regulations of the Game* (Jaques, 1864, and almost annually thereafter to 1870)

Lauthier, Joseph, *New Rules for the Jeu de Mail* (Delaulne, 1717; translated (in part) by Dr Prior, and by James Cunningham for A Lang)

Lillie, Arthur, *The Book of Croquet: its Tactics, Laws & Mode of Play* (Jaques, 1872)

——, *Croquet, its History, Rules & Secrets* (Longmans, 1897)

Locock, C D, *Modern Croquet Tactics* (Holmesdale Press, 1907)

Miller, David and Thorp, Rupert, *Croquet and How To Play It* (Faber, 1966)

Neal, John, *Croquet and Billiards* (Steam Printing Works, 1868–70)

Ormerod, G L, *Know the Game: Croquet* (Educational Productions 1961; A & C Black, 1985; a booklet available from the CA)

Osborn, Jack and Kornbluth, Jesse, *Winning Croquet* (Simon & Schuster, 1983; a book on croquet in America, in its 6 and 9-wicket forms; available from USCA)

Peel, W H, (ed), *The Association Laws of Croquet* (Jacques, 1895)

Prichard, D M C, *The History of Croquet* (Cassell, 1981; an exhaustive history of the game, with special reference of the Croquet Association; available from the CA)

Prior, R C A, *Notes on Croquet and some Ancient Bat and Ball Games related to it* (Williams & Norgate, 1872)

Reckitt, Maurice Benington, *Croquet Today* (MacDonald, 1954)

Reid, Captain Mayne, *Croquet* (Skeet, 1863; reprinted New York, 1869)

Routledge, Edmund, *Routledge's Handbook of Croquet* (Routledge, 1864)

Solomon, John, *Croquet* (Batsford, 1966; E P Publishing, 1983; a book on how to play croquet by a master of the game, available from the CA)

Tollemache, Lord, *Croquet* (Stanley Paul, 1914)

——, *Croquet: Hints on Practice, Tactics & Stroke Play* (Phillipson & Golder, 1926)

——, *Modern Croquet: Tips and Practice* (Strange, Eastbourne, 1947)

Tucker, G D R, *Some Croquet Verses* (Longmans, 1937)

Whitmore, Walter Jones, *Croquet Tactics* (Horace Cox, 1868)

Wylie, Keith, *Expert Croquet Tactics* (Privately published, 1986; available from Keith Wylie, 17 Carlton Crescent, Southampton, England)

Croquet Association publications

The Laws of Association Croquet and Golf Croquet, and the Regulations for Tournaments (The Croquet Association, 1984)

Neal, B G, *Basic Laws of Croquet* (Croquet Association)

INDEX

INDEX

Page numbers in *italics* refer to photographs or illustrations

Africa xvii, 34–5, 63, 104–6
Alaska Croquet Club 40
Aldershot tournament 22
Alice's Adventures Under Ground
    (Carroll) 31, 77, *78*
All England Croquet Club
    (AECC) 21–2, 47
All England Croquet and Lawn
    Tennis Club 47
All England Lawn Tennis and
    Croquet Club 48
America *see* USA
America, Central and South 94
American 'backyard' croquet
    165–7, *166*
American Roque League 39
American Rules *see* USCA
Anna Karenina (Tolstoy) 77–8
Antrim, Lady 4
*Appleton's Journal of Popular
    Literature, Science and Art* 39
arches 28, *28*
artificial court surfaces 103

artists 79–82
ash wood 33, 96, 122, 124
Aspinall, Nigel 40, 66, 100, 125,
    129, 144, 164; wins 64, *64,
    100*, 102
'Aunt Emma' play xix, 12–13,
    152, 164
Australia xvii, 36, 54, 101, 117,
    168
Ayres equipment 28, 51, 53

'backyard' croquet 35, 165–7,
    166
balls: colour sequence 6, 127,
    160, 163, 164, 172–3;
    materials 24, 32, 108, 109, 121
Barkworth, Peter 74
beechwood 124
Benetfink's equipment 51
Bent grasses 107
Bermuda 163
'bisque' 153–4, 162
Bobadilla, Enrique de 35

Bon Vivant Club (Illinois) 106, 149
boules 93
Bournemouth Pavilion Theatre 72
boxwood 33, 95, 97; balls 24, 32, 121
breaks 144-9, *145–6, 147–8*, 151, 175
British Croquet Association *see* Croquet Association
British Library xv, 23
British Museum 7
British standard grip 129, *130*
Brownlow, Mr James 4
Buckland, Frank 22
Budding, Edwin 104
Budleigh Salterton Club 99
Burchfield, Archie 40

Calladine, C. R. 138
Cambridge University 74
Campbell, Mrs Octavia Helen 4
Canada 36
cannon 135, 138
Carlisle, Hugh *116*
Carlisle, Veronica xix, 66, 67, 100, 106, 160
Caro sculpture 74
Carroll, Lewis 13, 31, 77, 78, 91, 169, 173
Cassiobury Park (Hertfordshire) 22
Chastleton House xv, 14–23 *passim*, *20*
Chaucer, Geoffrey 10
Cheltenham Club 99, 100
chess 89, 91
Chesterton, G. K. 78
China 36, 37

Churchill, Sir Winston xviii
clips 24, 109, 121–2
club, joining a 98–9
Clutton-Brock, Professor Alan xv, 16, 17, 18, 19, 21
Clutton-Brock, Barbara xv, 17
Clutton-Brock, Emma *née* Hill 12–13
Clutton-Brock, Tom 12
coaching 101
Colchester Club 100, 101
Colchester-Wemyss, Sir Francis 56
Collin, Mary 66
Complete Croquet Player, The (Heath) 31, 108
computer game 168
Connery, Sean 72
Contemplating Croquet (Sproat sculpture) 82
Cooke, Nathaniel 91
Corbally, Cyril 48
Costa Rica 163
Cotter, Patrick xviii, 60
courts (lawns) 44–5, 66, 103–9, 117–20, *119*
'Cowardly Tactics' (Lillie) 12
Cox, Horace 14
'Cozzare' 53
cricket 8–9
'crinoline croquet' *11*, 26
'Crokey' 168
croquet: etymology 8–10; taking xvii, 133, 139, 151, 164
Croquet (magazine) 63, 102, 110, 138, 164
Croquet (Reid) 23
Croquet (Sloan painting) 82
Croquet (Tissot painting) 79, *81*
Croquet (Tollemache) 51

Croquet Association (CA) 101,
  102, 124, 162, 168; Laws *see*
  Laws; membership 36, 48, 53,
  58, 64; officials xv, xviii, 56,
  98–9, 105, 153; and Sports
  Council 55, 63
'croquet castles' 169–73, *171*
Croquet Foundation of America
  40
Croquet Gazette 34, 48, *49*, 53, 63,
  76
Croquet and How to Play It (Miller
  & Thorp) 138
Croquet International 40
*Croquet: Its History, Rules and
  Secrets* (Lillie) 3
*Croquet, the Laws and Regulations
  of the Game* (Jaques) 29–31,
  118
Croquet à Mezy (Morisot
  painting) 79
Croquet Nonsense (Crowther-
  Smith) *52*
Croquet Party (Kaemmerer
  painting) 79
Croquet Player, The (Wells) 78
'Croquet Queen' (illustration)
  25, 26
Croquet Tactics (Whitmore) 14,
  19, 21
Croquet Today (Reckitt) 113
Croquet Up to Date (Lillie) 12,
  50, *50*
crowns 120, 122
Crowther, Leslie 73
Crowther-Smith, H. F. 52, 53
Cumberland turf 104

Davidson, Mrs 33
Deane, Mr Justice Bargrave 74–5

Dell'Ottonaio, Giovanni 7
Devonshire Park tournament
  116
Diéz, Angeles 35
Disraeli, Benjamin 16, 29, 76–7
Dodgson, Irene 91
double-banking 160
doubles 63, 71–2, 159–60
'Doxil' 51
D'Oyly Carte Opera Company
  72
dress 28–9, 48, 68–9, 113–16,
  114, 115
drive 135, *136*
Duffield, Edward 101
'Duralon' 125

Eastbourne Club 100
Eastwood-house 68
'Eclipse' balls 121
'Eclipse' mallet 97
Eglinton Castle 28
Egypt 35, 104–6
'either ball game' 127, 164
Elphinstone-Stone, Lydia 59
Engineering (magazine) 138
England 3–10, 28–9, 42, 50, 53,
  91, 101; teams and players xix,
  54, 55, 60, 113
Essex, Lord and Lady 22, 28
Evesham tournament 20
Expert Croquet Tactics (Wylie)
  143

faults 141
Fearnley-Whittingstall, Mrs
  Alice Mary 74
Fescues grasses 107
Field, The 14, 20, 21, 22, 31, 77,
  122

First World War 53, 54
Forster equipment 42
France 4, 11, 35

Gabor, Zsa Zsa 43
Gaekwar of Baroda, Maharajah
    34, *34*
Game of Croquet (Homer
    painting) *80*
Game of Croquet (Nash
    watercolour) *82*
'Game of War' 16, 19, 23
Garbo, Greta 78
'gate ball' 36
Georgia Croquet Club 43
Germany 35
Gezira Club (Cairo) 35, 104–6
Girls' Own Paper 69
Godby, Robin 35
Godfree, Kitty 67
Goldwyn, Samuel 40
golf croquet 72, 162–3
'Gossima' 91
Gower, Lilias 50, 51
Granada Television 102
Grand National Croquet Club
    22, 23
grasses 35, 107
Graves, Mr 104
Great Britain 35, 55, 98, 101,
    164, 168; England 3–10, 28–
    9, 42, 50, 53, 91, 101; (teams
    and players) xix, 54, 55, 60,
    113; Northern Ireland 37;
    Scotland 28, 36, 101; Wales
    37, 101
Great Exhibition (1851) 6, 29
Greene King brewers 102
grip 60, 123, 129, *129, 130, 131*

Hale, J. H. 47
Hale setting 47, 126, 127
hammer shot, 132, 135
handicaps: 126, 153–4, 156; in
    doubles 63, 71–2, 159–60
Hands, Paul 147
'Happy Families' 89, 91
'Hard Lines' 23
Harriman, Averell, xviii, 40
Harris, Rolf 74
Hart, Moss xix, 40
Heath, Dunbar Isidore 31
Heath, James Dunbar 31, 108
Heyman, Jacques 138
hickory wood 122, 123–4
Hicks, Humphrey 56, *57*, 107
Highgate tournament *69*
Hill, Thomas 79
Hinge and Bracket 73
Homer, Winslow 39, 79, 80
'hoopitis' 61
hoops: materials 109, 120, 126;
    number 44–5, 126; sequence
    127; size 21, 28, 32, 33, 36, 70,
    120
Hoy, Bill and Becky 43
Hunstanton club 100
Hurlingham Club 61, 67, 98, 99,
    100, 101, 104, 106–7
Hyde White, Wilfred 74

Ilchester, Lord 22
Illustrated London News 36, 37, 91
'Imperial Chinese Game of
    Frogs and Toads' 17, 23
India 32–4, 38
indoor croquet 167–8
International Challenge Cup
    Tournament 35
International Croquet Ball 40

International Herald Tribune 74
International Laws *see* Laws
Ireland 3–4, 5, 35, 48, 101;
    Northern 37
Irish grip 123, 129, *131*
Irish peel 154
Irish stance 48
Italy 7, 11

Jamaica 162
Japan 36, 101
Jaques, Christopher *92*, 93, 94
Jaques, John, & Son 5, 89–97,
    109; catalogues: (1910) 53, 96,
    97; (1931) *110*; croquet
    equipment: (early) 23–4, 28,
    32, 33, 58, 122; (modern) 34–
    6, 42, 96, *121*, 124–5, 169;
    parlour games 16, 17, 168
Jaques, John I 90, 91, *92*
Jaques, John II 3, 5, 90–1, *92*;
    on laws and regulations 6, 14,
    21, 29–31, 108
Jaques, John III 91
Jaques, John IV 91, 93
Jaques, John V *92*
Jaques, Thomas 89–90
Jarden, Jean 66
Jerez de la Frontera Club 35
Jones, Henry 'Cavendish' 47
Jourdan, Louis xviii
jump shot 132, 134–5, 163

Kaemmerer painting 79
Karlock, Merlin 149
Kaufman, George S. 40
Keating, H. F. R. 78–9
Kentucky Croquet Association
    39

'Kingball' 51, 169
Kingston-upon-Thames club 99

Land and Water 22
Lane, General 33
Lauthier, Joseph 121
Law, Arthur 56
lawn tennis 34, 45–8, 54, 162
Lawn Tennis (magazine) 48
Lawn Tennis and Croquet
    (magazine) 48
lawns *see* courts
Lawrence, Sir John 32
laws, early 3–6, 14, 21, 23, 29–
    31, 44, 47, 77, 108
Laws of Association Croquet,
    'International' xvii, 35, 36,
    126; examples 101, 106, 137,
    141, 150, 153, 155, 158, 161,
    164; *see also* Appendix B
leaves 149–50, *150*, 155, 157
Leech, John 26, 27
lignum vitae 24, 33, 94–5, *95*,
    123, 124
Little, Arthur 3, 5, 19–20, 21, 26,
    28, 32–3; *Croquet Up to Date*
    12, 50
Lloyd Pratt, Bryan 62–3
Locock, C. D. 51
Longman, Mrs 48
Longman, Willie 58
Longworth Cup 59
Lorris, Guillaume de 10
Lothair (Disraeli) 29, 76–7
'Ludo' 89
Lynn, Vera 72

Mackenzie, Sir Compton xviii
Macmillan, Brian xv
Macnaghten, Miss 4, 5

MacRobertson Shield 36, 54–5,
    55, 60, 66
malacca wood 122
mallets *9*, 10, *97, 123*, 127;
    holding *see* grip; materials 33,
    38, 51, 96, 109–10, 122–5;
    (ivory) 3, 32, 93; (lignum) 94–
    5, 123, 124; shape 50, 73, 123,
    124–5; size 21, 28, 32, 36, 70,
    122–3, 124
'Maltese Cross Croquet' 51
Manet, Edouard 79, 80
'Mangola' 23
March, Frederic 78
Martin, Millicent 74
Marx, Harpo xviii
Mathews, Duff 48, 113
Meade, Miss 72, 73
Meadow Club (Long Island)
    106
Meadow grasses 107
'Mechanics of the Game of
    Croquet' (Calladine and
    Heyman) 138
Memorial Court (Cambridge) 74
Mexico 163
Miller, David 138
Milligan, Spike 72, 73
Modern Croquet Tactics (Locock)
    51
Mordaunt, Miss 23
Moreton family 68
Moreton-in-Marsh tournament
    20
Morisot, Berthe 79
Morning Chronicle 18
Mulliner, Stephen xviii, *156*
Muntz, G. A. 20
Museum of London 7
Music Hall 26, 82–6

Nailsea Club 99
Nash, John 82
National Croquet Club (NCC)
    22
National Trust 102
Neal, Bernard xviii, 60, 99, 124,
    129, 164; on Laws and tactics
    36, 106, 126, 136, 147, 161
New Zealand xvii, 36, 54, 103,
    114, 156, 168
'nine wicket' game 158
Northern Ireland 37
Notes of Croquet (Prior) 5
Nottingham Club 99

Olympic Games (1904) 39
openings 142–4, *143*
Original Invitational Cosmic
    Croquet Fantasmajoric
    Boogie 43
Osborne, Jack 36, 39, 40, *41*, 53,
    124
Oxford English Dictionary,
    Shorter 8
Oxford University 31

pall-mall 6–8, *7, 8,* 121
Palm Beach (Florida) 40, 42, 43,
    106
Palo Alto Spring (painting by
    Hill) 79
Parker, Allen 168
Parker, Dorothy 40
parlour croquet 167
Partie de Croquet (Manet
    painting) *80*
Pattison, Mark 20, 31
Peel, W. H. 20, 22, 124, 154
Peel mallet 124
Peel Memorial tournament 116

peeling 154–7, 161, 162
pegging out 26, 126, 140, 150–
    1, 155, 159, 174; in 'backyard'
    croquet 167; in short croquet
    162; in three-sided croquet
    169
pegs 109, 118, 120, 127, 163;
    number 28, 44, 126
Pepys, Samuel 8
Perfect Game, The (Chesterton) 78
'Permali' 124
Piggott's equipment 51
'Ping Pong' 89, 91
'Pirates' 169
poetry 13, 18–19, 25–6, 76, 86,
    107
Pollock, Henry 3
practice 151–2, 175
Prentis, Teddy xviii, 36
President's Cup 58, 64, 65, 120,
    156
Prichard, D. M. C. xv, 5, 18
Prince, John 156
Prior, Dr Richard 3, 5, 8–11, 13,
    22, 31, 44–5, 48
professionalism xviii, 59, 102
Prossor's equipment 51
Punch 13, 107; cartoons 26, *27,
    33*

Reckitt, Maurice 56, 76, 79, 113–
    16
Red Cross parcels 93
refereeing xviii
Reid, Captain Mayne 23–6, 122
repairs to mallets 109–10
Richmond, Duke of 70
Robertson, Sir Macpherson 54
'Rocker' mallet 97
Roehampton Club 48, 61, 101

roll 135, 136–7, *137*, 151
'roque' 39
roquet: etymology 10; making a
    xvii, 4, 132, 139, 151, 159,
    164, 169
Ross, Alan 10
Ross, F. Fraser 138
Ross, J. T. C. 31, 32, 34
Rothwell, Richard 35, 48, 53,
    104, *105*, 113
Round Island Mallet Club
    (Connecticut) 40
Round Table group (New York)
    39
rovers 140, 150–1, 159, 163, 164,
    167, 169
Royal Ballet School 101
rules *see* Laws
running a hoop 132, 133–4, *134*,
    139, 151, 162–3, 164, 169
rush 132–3, *133*
Rush on the Ultimate, A (Keating)
    78–9
Ryegrasses 107

Saifuddien, Sir Omar Ali 34
Santa Barbara Croquet Club 36
scoring 140–1, 163
Scotland 28, 36, 101
Scotsman, The 18
Scott, Clement 86
season 101–2
Second World War 58, 91, 93
short croquet 63, 66, 117, 161–2
shots: types 132–8; sequence
    139–40
Sinden, Donald xviii
Singapore 36
Skowhegan equipment 42
Slazenger, Mr 48

Sloan, John 82
Small House at Allington, The
   (Trollope) 76
'Snakes and Ladders' 89
Solomon, Eric 125
Solomon, John 56, 58, *58*, 59–
   62, *61*, 101, 103, 123; on Laws
   and tactics 127, 132, 138, 142,
   155–6
Solomon grip 60, 129, *130*
Solomon mallet 123–4
South Africa xvii, 35, 63
South African Croquet
   Association 35
Southwick Club 99, 100, 101
Spain 35
Spencer Ell, Montague 56, 58,
   58
Spencer Ell Cup 58
sphairistike 45–7
split shot 135, 137–8, *138*, 151
Spong, A. H. E. 48
Sports Council 55, 63, 99
Spratt, Mr 4–5, 29
Sproat, Christopher 82
'Squails' 16–17, *17*, 23
stalking 131–2
stance (style) xvii, 48, 128, *128*
standard grip 129, *129, 130*
Staunton, Howard 91
Steel, Dorothy Dyne 51, *52*, 60
Steel Bowl 66
stop shot 135–6, *136*, 151
style (stance) xvii, 48, 128, *128*
'Sunrise' (Caro sculpture) 74
Surbiton Club 99
Surrey Cup 58
Sweden 35
Switzerland 35
Swope, Herbert Bayard 39–40

'Table Croquet' *51*, 53, 168
'Table Tennis' 91
Tactical Games of Ely 168
tactics 4, 29, 142–52, 155, 159,
   174–5
take-off 135, *136*, 137
Taylor, Liz *65*
television coverage 36, 102, 161–
   2
Tenniel, John 77, 91
tennis 34, 45–8, 54, 162
Test matches 54, 56
Thorp, Rupert 138
three-sided croquet 64, 169
'Tiddley Winks' 89
'tight croquet' 4, 28, 29–31, *30*
Tiller girls 74
time limits 159
Tingey, Robert 105
Tippett, Sir Michael xviii
Tissot, J. J. J. 79, 81
Tollemache, Lord 51, 60, 131
Tolstoy, Leo 77–8
Townsend, Ken 109
Trollope, Anthony 76

United All England Croquet
   Association 48
US Croquet Hall of Fame Ball
   40
US standard grip *129*
USA 24, 38–43, 54, 101, 124,
   168; croquet art 79, 82;
   croquet variations 39, 158,
   160, 165–7; Florida xviii, 35,
   40, 42, 43, 106; Illinois 149,
   106; New York 39, 106
USCA (United States Croquet
   Association) 38–9, 40, 162;
   National Championships 40,

42; Official Rules xvii, 35, 36,
    127, 159, 163–5, 167
USSR xviii, 36

'Vaccination on Parnassus'
    (Whitmore) 18–19
'Venetian' mallet 96, 97

Wales 37, 101
Walker Croquet Equipment 125
Walsh, J. H. 21, 31, 47
War Department 93
Webber Footballs 93
Webster, Fred 'Spider' 91
Wells, H. G. 78
West Indies 36, 163
Wharrad, Lionel xviii, *63*, 161
Wheeler, Dr Roger *116*
Whichelo variation 155
Whitmore, Walter Jones xv, 6,
    12-23, *15*, 44, 47, 77, 122, 174
Whitmore-Jones, Louisa 18
Whitmore-Jones, Mary 12, 16,
    18, 23
Whitmore-Jones, William 17
Whitmore-Jones, Wolryche
    (brother of Walter) 16, 18, 23

Whitmore-Jones, Wolryche
    (uncle of Walter) 14–15
'wickets' 39, 165
Wiggins, Susan 66
Williams, Mr Bange 24
Willis, C. E. 126
Willis setting 126
Wimbledon 22, 44, 47–8, 162;
    Lawn Tennis Museum 45, 48,
    104
Wingfield, Walter Clopton 45–7
winter croquet 160
wires 120, 122
Woking Club 53
Women's Championship 67
Woollcott, Alexander 40
World Croquet Federation 164
World Games 101
Worthing Club 99
Wylie, Keith 40, 55, 56, 59, *59*,
    62, 101; on Laws and tactics
    143, 149, 155–6

Yorke Batley, Mrs Frances 72–4

Zambia 35
Zanuck, Darryl F. xix, 40